BELL'S CATHEDRALS:
THE CATHEDRAL CHURCH OF ELY

LECTOR HOUSE PUBLIC DOMAIN WORKS

BELL'S CATHEDRALS:
THE CATHEDRAL CHURCH OF ELY

WALTER DEBENHAM SWEETING

ISBN: 978-93-90314-23-2

Published: 1910

LECTOR HOUSE LLP
E-MAIL: lectorpublishing@gmail.com

ELY CATHEDRAL FROM THE SOUTH.

BELL'S CATHEDRALS:
THE CATHEDRAL CHURCH OF ELY

A HISTORY AND DESCRIPTION OF THE BUILDING WITH A SHORT ACCOUNT OF THE FORMER MONASTERY AND OF THE SEE

BY

THE REV. W. D. SWEETING, M.A.

VICAR OF HOLY TRINITY, ROTHERHITHE
AND AUTHOR OF "PETERBOROUGH"

THE ARMS OF THE SEE

WITH XLVII ILLUSTRATIONS

1910

AUTHOR'S PREFACE.

It is hardly necessary to give a complete list of all the authorities consulted in the preparation of this book. As specially valuable for Ely may be named the "Liber Eliensis" and the "Inquisitio Eliensis"; the histories of Bentham, Hewett, and Stewart; the "Memorials of Ely," and the Handbook to the Cathedral edited and revised by the late Dean; Professor Freeman's Introduction to Farren's "Cathedral Cities of Ely and Norwich"; and the various reports of Sir G. G. Scott. But numerous other sources of information have been examined, and have supplied facts or theories; and in nearly every instance, particularly where the very words are quoted, the authority is given in the text or in the notes.

My best thanks are due to the Dean of Ely for his ready courtesy in allowing free access to every part of the cathedral and for his solution of various difficulties which had presented themselves in comparing different accounts of the fabric. I have also to thank the Rev. T. Perkins and the Photochrom Company for the use of the photographs from which the illustrations have been prepared. For many curious details, and for the loan of some books that are out of print and difficult to obtain, I acknowledge my obligation to Mr. C. Johnson, of Ely.

W. D. SWEETING.

CONTENTS

LIST OF ILLUSTRATIONS

THE NORTH SIDE OF THE CATHEDRAL.

THE CATHEDRAL FROM THE SOUTH.

CHAPTER I.

THE HISTORY OF THE BUILDING.

No mention has been found of Ely as a town before the time of the virgin queen S. Etheldreda. The district known as the Isle of Ely—which now includes the whole of the northern part of Cambridgeshire above the River Ouse, together with a few parishes east of that river that are in the county—is spoken of at the time of the marriage of the princess as if it were a district well known and perhaps of some importance, as it was assigned to her as a dowry. Some writers have held that the expression the Isle of Ely applied only to the rising ground on which the city now stands and to its immediate neighbourhood. If this were ever the case, the name was soon used for a larger district. In the "Liber Eliensis" the limits of the isle are given as seven miles in length by four in breadth, while the extent of the two hundreds belonging to Ely reaches from Tydd to Upware and from Bishop's Delf to Peterborough. We have many examples of large inland districts where a series of rivers has happened to isolate them being known as isles. The Isles of Athelney, Axholme, Purbeck, Thanet, are familiar instances. Perhaps the town is more likely to take its name from the district than the district from the town. It will be seen that in none of the examples just given is the name derived from a town. We have the authority of Bede for the statement that Ely (*Elge*) was a region containing about six hundred families, like an island (*in similitudinem insulæ*), and surrounded by marshes or waters.

When told that Ely means the "Island of Eels," many persons suppose this to be a fanciful etymology, and smile at the idea; but the best authorities are agreed that this is the true derivation of the name.[1] A suggestion that the willow-trees, so abundant in the region, gave the name (Celtic, *Helyg*) has met with some support. A third suggestion, that the word comes from the Greek for a "marsh," hardly deserves mention. The Saxon word for "eel" was apparently pronounced exactly as the modern word. Bede gives this etymology: "A copia anguillarum, quæ in iisdem paludibus capiuntur, nomen accepit." William of Malmesbury, in his "Gesta Pontificum," 1125, takes the same view. The "Liber Eliensis," of about the same date, also adopts it. Milton may not be regarded as a great authority upon such a question; he writes, however, as considering the matter settled. In his Latin poem on the death of Bishop Felton, of Ely, who died in 1626, he says that Fame, with her hundred tongues, ever a true messenger of evil and disaster, has spread the report of the bishop's death:

> "Cessisse morti, et ferreis sororibus,
> Te, generis humani decus,
> Qui rex sacrorum fuisti in insulâ
> Quæ nomen Anguillæ tenet."

That Ely should mean "Isle of Eels," and that the expression Isle of Ely is consequently redundant, is no argument against this view. The Isle of Athelney, beyond all question, means the Isle of the Æthelings' Isle. Compare also a remarkable instance of redundancy in the name of the Isle of Axholme. This name, says Canon Taylor, "shows that it has been an island during the time of the Celts, Saxons, Danes, and English. The first syllable, *Ax*, is the Celtic word for the water by which it was surrounded. The Anglo-Saxons added their word for island to the Celtic name, and called it Axey. A neighbouring village still goes by the name of Haxey. The Danes added *holm*—the Danish word for island—to the Saxon name, and modern English influences have corrupted Axeyholme into Axelholme, and contracted it into Axholme, and have finally prefixed the English word *Isle*."[2]

The North Girvii and the South Girvii were two peoples that formed districts of the East Anglian kingdom. In the early part of the seventh century Anna was King of the East Angles; and Etheldreda, his daughter, was born at Exning, near Newmarket,—a Suffolk parish, but detached from the main county and entirely surrounded by Cambridgeshire,—about the year 630. When quite young there were many suitors for her hand, but she was altogether unwilling to accept any one of them. But the king, her father, had so high an opinion of Tonbert—one of the noblemen of his Court, who was alderman, or, as some render it, prince, of the South Girvii—that he prevailed upon his daughter to be married to him, and the marriage took place in 652, two years before Anna's death. From her husband Etheldreda received the Isle of Ely—that is, the whole of the region of the South Girvii—as a marriage settlement ("Insulam Elge ab eodem sponso ejus accepit in dotem"). It is clear, therefore, that Tonbert was something more than an officer of

---

[1] The origin of the name Ely has been discussed in "Fenland Notes and Queries," ii., pp. 316, 371.

[2] "Words and Places," 2nd ed., 1865, p. 355.

the king's if he had the power of assigning such a district to his wife.

Tonbert only lived for three years after his marriage, and at his death his widow came into possession of the Isle of Ely according to the terms of her marriage settlement. She resided within it, and gave herself up entirely to works of religion and devotion, entrusting the civil government of her territory to Ovin. Her reputation for piety was spread far and wide, and attracted the attention of Egfrid, son of Oswy, King of Northumberland, who sought her hand in marriage. But no attraction he could offer could persuade the princess to change her state, until her Uncle Ethelwold, who was now King of East Anglia, overcame her scruples. The disturbed state of his kingdom and the importance of an alliance with so powerful a house as that of Oswy are believed to have influenced Ethelwold to urge his niece to give her consent to the proposed marriage; and the marriage took place at York. It is constantly affirmed by all historians that in neither of these marriages did the married couple live together as man and wife. At the Northumbrian Court Etheldreda lived for twelve years, her husband meanwhile, in 670, having become king. He had been for some years previously associated with his father in the government. The queen, however, became more and more wearied of the glories of her royal position, and tired out her husband with persistent entreaties that she might be permitted to withdraw herself altogether from his Court and devote herself entirely to the religious life. At last she obtained his reluctant consent, and betook herself to Coldingham, where Ebba, the king's aunt, was abbess, and was there admitted into the order of nuns at the hands of Wilfrid, Archbishop of York. This Ebba was afterwards canonised, and her name is preserved in the name of the promontory on the coast of Berwickshire known as S. Abb's Head.

After remaining about a year at Coldingham, the queen found it necessary to move away. The king began to regret the permission he had given her, and, following the advice of some of his courtiers, made his way to the religious house where Etheldreda was settled, with the intention of forcibly compelling her return to his Court. His intention having become known to the abbess, she recommended the queen to escape at once to her own territory, the Isle of Ely. The queen immediately followed this advice. Egfrid arrived at Coldingham very soon after her departure, and set off in pursuit. No reason for her leaving Coldingham is given by Bede; but a lengthy account of the journey and its occasion is given in the "Liber Eliensis." In the remarkable sculptures on the corbels in the octagon are representations of two scenes that are unintelligible without this account; it is necessary, therefore, to summarise it here. Directly after setting out from Coldingham, which is some ten miles north of the Tweed, not far from the sea, the queen, with two lady companions, Sewenna and Sewara, reached a rocky eminence on the coast, where the king in pursuit came up with them; but he was "prevented from coming near them by a sudden and unusual inundation of water from the sea, which surrounded the hill, and continued in that state several days, without retiring into its former channel. Amazed at the strangeness of this appearance, the king presently interpreted it as the interposition of Heaven in her favour, and concluded that it was not the will of God that he should have her again; and this occasioned his retiring to *York* again, leaving the queen quietly to pursue her journey."[3] After the king had abandoned his intention of reclaiming his wife, the three ladies proceeded southwards, and crossed the Humber, and so through Winteringham and Alftham, where she stayed a few days, and where she is said to have built a church. This can only mean that she arranged for its building or undertook the cost. At West Halton, the next village to Winteringham (as Bentham has observed), the church is dedicated to S. Etheldreda; and this place may be identified with the Alftham of the chronicler. The party had now assumed the dress of pilgrims, and went by unfrequented roads, so as to escape observation. At one point of their journey a second miraculous event is recorded. The queen had lain down to sleep while her attendants kept watch, and had stuck her pilgrim's staff in the ground. When she awoke, this staff was found to have taken root and already to have brought forth leaves. It was left standing, and grew into a flourishing tree; and the place, from the circumstance, was named Etheldrede's-Stow.[4] A church was afterwards built and dedicated to S. Etheldreda.

In course of time the three pilgrims arrived safely at their destination. Wilfrid, the archbishop, soon joined them. He had lost favour with King Egfrid, being supposed to have influenced the queen in her decision to take the veil. The king, regarding his marriage with Etheldreda as being *de facto* dissolved, took another wife, who was for various reasons much opposed to Wilfrid. The archbishop also greatly resented the action of the king and Archbishop Theodore in dividing his diocese without his consent into four different sees, and he was at one time banished and at another imprisoned.

Etheldreda now set to work in earnest to establish a religious house. Her buildings were begun in 673. This year is accordingly taken as the date of the foundation of the monastery and of the town itself. King Ethelbert is indeed said to have built a church a short distance from the site of the present cathedral, at a place called Cratendune[5]; but there is much uncertainty as to the fact, and some considerable difficulties in reconciling the different references to it. It is stated that this church had but a short existence, being destroyed by Penda, King of Mercia. This Ethelbert was the Bretwalda, King of Kent, husband of the Christian queen Bertha. After his conversion he was instrumental in furthering the spread of Christianity among the East Saxons, and also apparently in East Anglia, one of the East Anglian kings, Redwald, having (but only for a time) given his adherence to the Christian religion. As the building of this church near Ely is stated to have been undertaken

---

[3] Quoted in Bentham, p. 52.

[4] This place has not been positively identified; but the general opinion is that Stow, about ten miles north-west of Lincoln, is the place. The existing church there is, however, dedicated to the Virgin Mary. It has been said that, besides Ely Cathedral, six ancient churches in England are dedicated to S. Etheldreda. In this number the ancient episcopal chapel in Ely Place and the destroyed church at Histon, Cambridgeshire, are probably not included. Other churches with this dedication occur at Guilsborough, Northamptonshire, West Halton, Lincolnshire, Bishop's Hatfield, Hertfordshire, Norwich, and S. Audrie's, in Somerset. The writer has not been able to discover the sixth. At Swaffham Prior, ten miles south of Ely, are the ruins of a small chapel with this dedication.

[5] A mile south is a field still known as Cratendon Field.

on the advice of Augustine, who died in 604, we have an approximate date for it, since Augustine only arrived in England in 597. Whether this church was so built by Ethelbert or not, it seems clear there was some church in a state of partial decay standing in 673, because it is recorded that at first Etheldreda designed to restore it and to make it the centre of her religious work; but the present site was judged to be more suitable, and there she began to build. The few remaining inhabitants of Cratendune soon abandoned their dwellings, and came to live near the rising buildings of the monastery.

Upon the death of King Anna, who fell in battle against Penda, King of the Mercians, he was succeeded in turn by his brothers Adelbert and Ethelwold, and the kingdom then went to Adulphus, Anna's son and Etheldreda's brother. He greatly assisted his sister in raising the buildings of her monastery, contributing considerably to the cost; but the plans and arrangements are thought to have been designed by Wilfrid, who is known to have spent much time at Ely. It was he who gave his benediction when Etheldreda was formally instituted as abbess, and who admitted the earliest members of the house. As was not unusual, the society included monks as well as nuns. In later times the Benedictine rule was adopted. In the very year of the foundation, possibly on account of its royal foundress and the support of the king, her brother, the special privilege of exemption from interference, either by king or bishop, was assigned to it in a national assembly. This at least seems to be the meaning of the decree, as given in "Liber Eliensis," that with respect to the Isle of Ely, now dedicated to God's service, "Non de Rege nec de Episcopo libertas loci diminueretur, vel in posterum confringeretur."

To endow and provide for her monastery, the foundress assigned her entire principality of the isle. In this way the temporal power, which was afterwards so peculiar a feature in the privileges of the bishops, was acquired. In about five years Wilfrid went to Rome to obtain the Papal confirmation of the grants and liberties of the new foundation; but Etheldreda did not live to see his return. She died of some contagious disease, June 23, 679, in the seventh year after she had become abbess. She was buried, by her own directions, not in the church, but in the nuns' graveyard. She was certainly not fifty years of age at the time of her death. As will be seen hereafter, her body was removed into the church in the time of her successor.

No description is extant of the buildings of the monastery first erected. We know that the present cathedral is on the same site. Nor has any record been preserved of any discoveries that may have been made in later times, when extensive operations must have necessitated the laying bare of some of the original foundations. From what is known of some contemporary monasteries, we may conclude that the church at least was of stone. Not a fragment of it is known to be in existence at the present day. Whatever may have been its extent, it was wholly destroyed by the Danes in 870. For four years the Danes had been ravaging the eastern part of the country, burning monasteries and slaying their inmates. In the immediate district, Crowland and Thorney, Medeshamstede (Peterborough), and Ramsey had already felt the severity of their attack; crumbling walls alone remained where their destructive violence had been experienced. On their first attack on Ely they were repulsed. The advantages of the situation among the fens had already suggested the formation of something very similar to the famous Camp of Refuge in the eleventh century; and the force thus collected was sufficient to drive the Danes to their ships. But before long they returned with greater numbers, headed by one of their kings, most likely Hubba, and altogether overcame the resistance of the people of the isle. The conquerors then marched "directly to the Monastery of *S. Etheldreda*, at *Ely*, broke their way into it, and put all the Religious to the sword, as well the Nuns as the Monks, and others belonging to it, without any respect to age, sex, or condition; and after they had stript the Monastery of every thing that was valuable, and plundered the town, they set fire to the Church and all the buildings and houses; and went away loaded with the spoils, not only of the Town and Monastery of Ely, but likewise the chief effects and riches of the country round about, which the inhabitants of those parts had brought with them, as to a place of security."[6]

The destruction of Ely monastery in 870 and its resuscitation by King Edgar in 970 are an almost exact repetition of what took place at Peterborough. But there is a difference in the history of the interval. In the case of Peterborough, as far as is known, the ruin was complete, and not the smallest attempt was made for a hundred years either to restore the buildings or to revive the society. But at Ely, though the destruction was hardly less complete, we read that within a few years eight of the inmates of the monastery who had escaped when the place was burnt came back, and to a certain extent continued the establishment. They effected a partial restoration of a small portion of the church, and performed divine service. It is said that King Alfred, who succeeded in expelling the Danes, acquiesced in these clerks thus taking possession of the place, although the former King of Mercia, finding the monasteries deserted, had annexed all their property. It does not appear certain whether these clerks were actual monks of the old monastery or clergy of the place; but the new society thus inaugurated was like a college of secular clergy. They were so far recognised as a settled establishment that new endowments were acquired from various benefactors.

The latter part of the tenth century was a time of great activity in founding monasteries and in restoring those that had fallen into decay. Edgar, the king, Dunstan, Archbishop of Canterbury, and Ethelwold, Bishop of Winchester, were all enthusiastic in the work. The advancement of the monastic system was the great object they all had at heart. Application was made to the king by two nobles about his Court, both foreigners, for a grant of the Isle of Ely, lately the possession of the monastery. It does not appear what services either had rendered to warrant the application. The sheriff of the county, however, interfered to prevent any such grant being made. He represented to the king the true state of affairs—in what way the Isle of Ely had become the property of the monastery, how all had been lost after the Danish invasion, and in what a lamentable condition the place was at the time, although the remains of the sainted abbesses were still on the spot. The king immediately saw here a new opportunity of furthering his religious work. Committing the details to Bishop Ethelwold, he authorised him to repair

---

[6] Bentham, p. 68.

the church, provide fresh monks (but no nuns), make arrangements for divine service, and supply new buildings for the new inmates. At the same time the king undertook to provide lands and revenues for the support of the monastery. When the bishop had discharged his commission he obtained from the king a new grant of the whole of the Isle of Ely for the restored monastery.

The charter of King Edgar is printed in the appendix to Bentham's "History and Antiquities." The king describes himself as "Basileus dilecte insule Albionis," and as desirous of shewing his gratitude for the peace secured after conquering the Scots, Cambrians, and Britons by restoring decayed monasteries and establishing them under the Benedictine rule; and in particular he desires to honour the monastery in the region of Ely (*Elig*), anciently dedicated to S. Peter, rendered famous by the relics and miracles of the renowned virgin Etheldreda, "who, with body uncorrupted, lasts even to this day in a white marble mausoleum." He appoints Brithnoth first abbot, and assigns certain lands and revenues, including ten thousand eels due to him as king, for the maintenance of the monastery. To signify the public character of the grant, it is stated in the attestation clause that it is made not in a corner, but in the open: "Non clam in angulo sed sub divo palam evidentissime." The charter is signed by the king, two archbishops, twelve bishops, the queen, eleven abbots, nine dukes (*duces*), and forty-one knights. This was in the year 970.

As has been said, the old establishment had given place to a company of secular clergy. These were dispossessed by Bishop Ethelwold, unless any chose to attach themselves to the new foundation upon the constitution of the Benedictine house. But during the century that had elapsed since the Danes evicted the monks, these clergy must have been careful custodians of the church and buildings, most likely restoring by degrees and erecting fresh accommodation as their means permitted, for there is no account of any considerable rebuilding by Bishop Ethelwold. Repairs and enlargement and decorations were necessary; but the bishop probably found everything nearly ready to his hands, and he was not required to undertake anything so extensive as had to be done under similar circumstances at Peterborough. Everything was duly prepared for the new monastery by the Feast of the Purification, 970; and on that day the church and buildings, some partly restored and some newly erected, were consecrated by Archbishop Dunstan.

During the time of Elsin, the second abbot (981-1016), some considerable improvements were effected by Leofwin (of whom more will be told in a later chapter) in the church. He rebuilt and enlarged the south aisle, joining it to the rest of the building. In one of its porches, or side-chapels (*in uno porticu*), he built an altar to the Virgin Mary, erecting over it a stately image of gold and silver, adorned with valuable jewels. It is probable that this chapel, and the one that possibly replaced it when the present cathedral was built, may have been colloquially known as the lady-chapel, for it is sometimes said that a lady-chapel was in existence before the fourteenth century; but there was nothing about it of the dignity and importance usually associated with the name.

Although the Isle of Ely plays so important a part in the history of the Norman Conquest, and was the scene of the last great stand made against the Conqueror, neither the party of Hereward and the Camp of Refuge, nor the forces of the king, did any material damage to the buildings of the monastery. Its affairs were indeed brought to confusion, as the monks had sided with Hereward, and the Conqueror gave orders for the plunder of all the goods of the monastery. But the monks purchased from the king his forgiveness, and the liberty of the place, and the restoration of what property had been taken away, for the sum of a thousand marks. To raise this amount they had to sell almost everything in the church of gold and silver; and the "Liber Eliensis" enumerates among precious objects thus alienated, crosses, altars, shrines, texts, chalices, patens, basins, brackets, pipes (*fistulas*), cups, salvers, and the image of the Virgin seated with her Son on a throne, which Abbot Elsin had wrought of gold and silver. It is true that most, if not all, of these were recovered in about ten years, for it is on record that the Norman abbot, Theodwin, refused to accept the abbacy until the king would restore what had been taken away. This seems to refer to the goods sold to raise the money demanded as the price of his forgiveness.

When the building of the existing cathedral was commenced there was not the same necessity as existed in many other cases. There was no ruin to be rendered serviceable. A church was actually standing and in constant use. It must therefore have been felt that the importance and wealth of the foundation demanded a more magnificent minster. When Simeon, the ninth abbot (1081-1093), was appointed, he found the property of the abbey still in an unsatisfactory state. Lands really belonging to it were in many instances held by powerful persons, who under various pretences defied the rights of the religious house. So the abbot's first work was to recover these. By help of the king's commission he was entirely successful. But while inquiries were being instituted, and proceedings for recovery were being taken, he conceived the design of erecting a very noble church, and set about laying the foundations of it. He could not, from his great age, have hoped to see much progress made, but he did live to see a very considerable portion completed. He devoted a great part of his private fortune, which was large, to the work. He began with the transepts. This is in itself sufficient to shew that there was a choir in use. The regular practice, when a wholly new church was to be built, was to commence at the east end. The lower part of both transepts is Simeon's work. It is of plain Early Norman character, and represents all that is now in existence of what he erected. From a slight increase in ornamentation in the capitals in the north transept, we infer that the actual commencement was made in the south transept. Of course these transepts were of four bays—not as at present, of three only—the bay in each case nearest the central tower having been destroyed when the tower fell. That tower was of Norman date, and is sometimes spoken of as Simeon's Tower. But he cannot have built the whole of it. If he raised it as high as the great supporting arches, which is of course possible, there must have been also supports in all the four adjacent portions of the church, reaching almost to the summit of the arches, so that he would have had to build at least one bay of the triforium and clerestory stages. If he did so, all such work perished with the fall of the tower. It is more probable that he raised the piers of the tower arches only a few feet higher than the main arcade of the transepts.

Abbot Simeon's successor, Richard (1100-1107), proceeded with the building. No abbot had been appointed by William II., and the works had consequently been suspended for seven years. Notwithstanding many troubles and distractions (he was actually deposed at a council at Westminster in 1102, though restored by Papal bull in the next year), Abbot Richard made great advance in the building of the church. He was only abbot for seven years. By 1106 he had finished the east end, which may have terminated in an apse as at Peterborough, and possibly the tower. On October 17 in that year the remains of Saints Etheldreda, Sexburga, Ermenilda, and Withburga were solemnly removed to the new choir, and re-interred in front of the high altar. For some reason not explained there was no such attendance of high ecclesiastical dignitaries as was usual on such occasions. The Bishop of Norwich, four abbots, and one archdeacon were all that could be found to attend the translation. The account is noteworthy because it describes the orderly processions from "the Old Church," and the taking the bodies thence one at a time, "with singing and praise into the New Church." We are not to conclude from this that the former church was on a different site. The new buildings were apparently quite close to the former, and possibly some part of the old church had already been pulled down as the new choir was being built, and the completion of the aisles of the choir would necessitate the pulling down of the remainder. But the remains of the foundress and others must first be removed to their new resting-place. Both Simeon and Richard, while urging on the church building, were by no means regardless of the domestic buildings of the monastery. These were being enlarged and improved at the same time. Two bays of the nave next to the tower were also the work of Abbot Richard.

Two years after the death of Abbot Richard the bishopric was constituted. The bishop henceforward was the abbot of the house, though the superintendence of the domestic concerns of the monastery devolved upon the prior. Until 1198 the bishops appointed the priors, but afterwards they were elected by the monks. There was naturally some difficulty in dividing fairly between the bishop and the monastery the peculiar rights which were attached to the government of the Isle of Ely; but all was amicably arranged. As part of the arrangement the bishops were discharged from all obligation to repair or sustain the fabric of the church. But numbers of the bishops did contribute largely to its building and embellishments; and henceforward the works carried on are assigned to the bishops holding office at the time.

By degrees, during the twelfth century, the building of the nave advanced. For upwards of sixty years we find no record in the chronicles of any specific work done at any particular time. When we come to Bishop Riddell (1174-1189) we read that he "carried on the new work and Tower at the West-end of the Church, almost to the top." How high this tower was we cannot tell. It was probably surmounted by a pyramid. A later bishop, Northwold (1229-1254), removed the original capping and built the existing Early English stage; so we conclude from the words: "Ipse construxit de novo turrim ligneam versus galileam ab opere cementario usque ad summitatem."

The first three bishops ruled for a period of eighty years. This seems too long a time to assign for the building of the nave, because there is so little difference in detail as we examine the work from east to west; and even when later work in a large building is purposely made to assimilate to what had been built some years before, the experienced eye can usually discover slight variations in mouldings or ornamentation which indicate something of a new fashion in architecture. Here we detect nothing of the sort. We can well understand how much reason there was at Ely why building work should have been in the twelfth century intermittent. The troublous times of Henry I. and Stephen were specially unfavourable to this place. Bishop Hervey, moreover, would have had but little time to devote to building. The complete constitution of the bishopric, the regaining possession of property that had been alienated in the time of Rufus, and the thorough establishment of his temporal jurisdiction over the isle took up all his time and energies. He was also constantly abroad in attendance on the king. In the next bishop's time the disaffected barons assembled in the Isle of Ely, and the bishop was of their party. The whole district was alternately in the hands of the king and of the barons. The property of the monastery suffered greatly by fines and exactions. The bishop himself was constantly moving about from place to place, and was many times compelled to make a hurried escape in fear of being apprehended by the king's party. When at last his peace was made with the king, his submission cost him three hundred marks. Neither his own resources nor those of the monastery were sufficient to raise this sum. Some of the treasures of the church had already been sold. Now the monks were persuaded to part with silver from S. Etheldreda's shrine and other valuable ornaments, in order to lend the bishop the sum he required. After the death of King Stephen there occurred a time of tranquillity. The bishop was advanced in dignity and became a Baron of the Exchequer. These various considerations make it at least very probable that no additions to the church of any importance were made until the reign of Henry II.; and, if so, we may come to the conclusion that the whole of the nave was built in his reign. The difference in the style of architecture between the Late Norman and the Transition to Early English is very noticeable as we look at the remaining portion of the west front, south of the galilee porch, the lower stages shewing no trace of anything but pure Norman, while above we see pointed arches, quatrefoils in circles, and other indications of the approaching change of style.

THE INTERIOR OF THE GALILEE BEFORE RESTORATION, C. 1817.

From Stevenson's Supplement to Bentham.

Bishop Eustace (1198-1215) made large additions to the fabric at his own expense. One sentence in the account of his work has given rise to much controversy:

"Ipse construxit a fundamento novam galileam ecclesiæ Eliensis versus occidentem sumptibus suis." Was this the Early English porch now known as the galilee? Some have thought that this name was bestowed upon the whole of the western transept, not including the porch. This is the view taken in recent years by Canon Stewart. He shews it was the current local opinion at the beginning of the eighteenth century. Dr. Tanner, who wrote the account of Ely in Browne Willis's "Mitred Abbies," takes this view, and speaks of the south arm of the transept as the "old Galilee" and the north arm as the "new Galilee." In the plan in Willis's "Survey of Cathedrals," 1727, the south part is described as the "South galilee, now the church workhouse," while on the north side we read, "Ruined part of Galilee." No doubt the character of the architecture is not inconsistent with the theory that the northern part may have been built or finished by Bishop Eustace, soon after he was appointed, in intentional imitation of the pronounced Norman work adjacent. Canon Stewart also points out that Bishop Eustace is known to have rebuilt S. Mary's Church, where the rough masonry and plain lancets are wholly unlike the beautiful work in the west porch. And he adds: "It is evident that Eustace had nothing to do with the erection of any part of the present cathedral. The galilee which he built has totally disappeared, and the porch which has gone under that name of late years must be the work of some unknown benefactor, who had probably seen Hugh de Northwold's presbytery, and determined to lengthen the church westward as it had been extended in the opposite direction."[7] The more generally received opinion, however, is that Bishop Eustace did really build what is now called the galilee. This is accepted by Bentham, Essex, and Miller, and more recently by Sir G. G. Scott.

No one can doubt that the entire west front, when standing, was much improved by the addition of this great porch. The front indeed never had the painfully flat appearance presented at some cathedrals, for its extreme length was not very great, and the projecting turrets at each end would greatly relieve the impression that it was the side, and not the end, of a building. But it requires something more than a tower in the centre of the front to give a true finish to a composition in which there runs at the top a single horizontal line from north to south. Richly traceried windows are not sufficient. Deeply recessed doorways are better; but here there was only one, of the nature of which we have no account. The great porch is exactly what was wanted.

In 1757 Essex recommended the removal of the galilee as being an encumbrance. The roof was ruinous, the walls were in bad condition; it was "neither ornamental nor useful"; it would cost a large sum to put it into decent repair. Happily this advice was not followed. In the course of the renovation then undertaken it was discovered that the remains of an older porch had been incorporated with the present one.

Bishop Northwold (1229-1254) commenced the building of the present presbytery.[8] There are now nine bays between the screen and the east end. The apse,

[7] "Architectural History of Ely Cathedral," 1868, p. 53.

[8] The presbytery, as the term is used at Ely, signifies the six eastern bays of the central portion of the church east of the transepts. The choir, or portion devoted to the daily choral

if such were the termination of the Norman church, was situated between what are now on each side the fourth and fifth piers from the screen. A line drawn from the west side of the fifth piers north and south would just touch the eastern end of the apse. Bishop Northwold pulled down the apse and one bay west of it, and extended the presbytery four more bays to the east, building in all six bays, of which two were included in the ritual choir, and four were to the east of the high altar. All this was done between the years 1235 and 1251. The bishop also erected a lofty timber spire on the west tower, which remained until the present Decorated stage was built.

We have no account of the consecration of the Norman choir. But after this extension of the building eastwards we read that the whole church was solemnly dedicated on September 17, 1252, in honour of Saints Mary, Peter, and Etheldreda. King Henry III. was present, as well as Prince Edward, afterwards king. When the new portion of the church was ready, the remains of the four saints were removed further east. In the Norman church the high altar was in the chord of the apse, assuming one to have been built; after Bishop Northwold's alterations it was placed at the east end of the present sixth bay, where the apse terminated. The shrine of the foundress was placed some feet further to the east, its eastern face standing about twelve feet in front of the existing altar.

This work of Bishop Northwold completed the plan of the cathedral as it now stands. The lady-chapel was indeed built afterwards, but that is to all intents and purposes a separate building. Nor is there any later thirteenth-century work in the church itself. The building operations of the second half of the century were confined to the domestic part of the monastery. As these were doubtless carried out by the convent from its own resources, there is little notice to be found of them in the records of the see. It is known that the rectory, now in the deanery grounds, belonged to this period. It was finished in the time of Prior Hemmingston (1274-1288).

The first half of the next century was a time of great and important work at the church. In 1321 the first stone of the lady-chapel was laid by Alan de Walsingham, the sub-prior, afterwards sacrist. It was finished in 1349; and though John of Wisbech had the charge of the erection, the sacrist having more important work to do at the church itself, we can hardly doubt that the designs were by Walsingham. The position of the lady-chapel, to the north-east of the north transept, is unique. At Bristol it is to the north of the north choir aisle. At Peterborough the lady-chapel (destroyed during the Commonwealth) was in a nearly similar situation, projecting eastward from the north transept. Whatever may have been the reason at Peterborough for this unusual position (some say that a public road close to the apse prevented an extension of the choir to the east), there is no necessity to question the accuracy of the explanation generally given of the site of the lady-chapel here—namely, that the place of honour, east of the high altar, was already appropriated to the shrine of S. Etheldreda.

---

service, varied in position from time to time.

THE SHRINE OF S. ETHELDREDA (FROM BENTHAM)

On the night of February 12, 1322, the eve of S. Ermenilda's day, the central tower fell. Its insecurity had long been known. The monks had just left their matin service in S. Catharine's Chapel. Some persons conclude from this fact that the choir had already been disused as being unsafe; but unless there is other evidence of this, the mere fact of the monastic matins being held in the chapel nearest to the domestic buildings seems hardly sufficient to justify the conclusion. The chapel here named was not (according to Dean Stubbs) the one now dedicated to S. Catharine at the west end of the cathedral, but one that adjoined the chapter-house. The fall of the tower destroyed three bays of the choir. Different opinions are held as to the character of the architecture of the bays thus destroyed. Some hold that Bishop Northwold built the choir and presbytery, from the central tower to the east end, in the Early English style, and that three of his bays were thrown down by the fall of the tower[9]; others think that the bays now ruined were part of the Norman work.[10] It is most probable that Northwold, designing to increase the length of the presbytery, only pulled down so much of the Norman work as was necessary for his purpose, leaving the western arches standing. This opinion is adopted in the account of his work given above. If this is correct, there would have been *four* Norman arches left standing between the tower and the Early English work. Of these, three on each side fell. When the new choir was constructed, the octagon taking up the space of the first bay, the fourth bay—presumably left un-

[9] See Murray's "Handbook," p. 198.
[10] See Hewett's "Brief History," p. 10.

injured—was removed, as being out of keeping between the Early English and the new Decorated bays; and hence three new bays were built, reaching to Bishop Northwold's work. All accounts agree that *three* bays were destroyed. But if both choir and presbytery were of Early English date, there must have been *four* bays overthrown, because the three Decorated bays now existing do not correspond in position to the three destroyed, for the present third bay from the screen is where the fourth bay was when the tower was standing.

No one could possibly have been found in the whole kingdom better qualified to cope with the great disaster that took place at Ely in 1322 than the officer of the house who had the special custody of the fabric. The originality and skill with which he designed and carried out the noble work that takes the place of the central tower, which is without a rival in the architecture of the whole world, are beyond all praise. The exquisite work in the lady-chapel would in itself have been sufficient to establish Walsingham's reputation as an architect of the very highest order of merit; but it would have revealed nothing, if it stood alone, of the consummate constructive genius which he displayed in the conception of the octagon. Of the design itself we shall speak hereafter. No time was lost in removing the mass of ruins; and we can imagine, as the ground was cleared and the grandeur of the opportunity gradually dawned upon Walsingham's mind, how he formed the design of dispensing with the four central pillars, and thereby securing eight instead of four for the support of his substitute for a central tower. At the same time the weight which these supports would have to bear was very much less than that of a massive tower of stone; so that there need be little fear of the fall of the lantern. Fergusson has pointed out that the roof of the octagon is the only Gothic dome in existence. Beresford Hope[11] compares the octagonal lanterns of Milan and Antwerp with that at Ely, which he calls unique in this country.

The building was begun as soon as the space was cleared. The stonework was finished in 1328, little more than six years after the tower fell. The woodwork of the vaulting and lantern took longer time; but this also was quite complete in 1342. Walsingham had become prior in the previous year. The weight of the lantern, it need hardly be said, is not borne, though it looks like it from below, by the vaulting that we see. There is a perfect forest of oak hidden from sight, the eight great angle posts being no less than 3 feet 4 inches by 2 feet 8 inches in section. There is also the leaden roof of the octagon (of that part which is exclusive of the lantern), 18 feet above the vaulting, to be supported. A glance at Plate 44 in Bentham's "History" gives some slight idea of the method of construction.[12]

---

[11] "The English Cathedral of the Nineteenth Century," 1861, p. 195.
[12] See also Dean Stubbs' "Historical Memorials of Ely Cathedral," pp. 151, 152.

THE OCTAGON ABOUT 1825.

From Wilds' English Cathedrals.

With such a man as Walsingham on the spot we cannot be wrong in assigning to him the authorship of all the architectural designs that were carried out in his lifetime. It is believed—for the date is not exactly known—that he died in 1364. Besides the lady-chapel and octagon, he must have designed the singularly beautiful bays of the presbytery between the octagon and Northwold's work. The exquisite way in which the main characteristics of the Early English work are adapted to the Decorated style demands our highest admiration. The arrangement of the three western bays on each side is exactly like Northwold's work, while the additional grace and beauty of ornamentation mark the advance in taste that distinguished the Decorated period. Bishop Hotham undertook the whole expense of rebuilding this portion of the cathedral. He did not live to see it completed, as he died in 1337, but he left money for the purpose. The total expense of this rebuilding is given at £2034 12*s*. 8¼*d*., while the cost of the octagon and lantern amounted to not very much more—£2406 6*s*. 11*d*. Nearly all this latter cost was defrayed by the monastery, little more than £200 having been contributed from external sources. These amounts must be multiplied by twenty, if not twenty-five, to represent the present value. The rebuilding of these three bays in the presbytery involved the rebuilding of the corresponding portions of the aisles.

The domestic buildings were also improved, and some new ones erected by Walsingham. "The Sacrist's Office he almost new built, made several additional apartments in it, and encompassed the whole with a strong wall; in the North-west corner of which he built a square building of stone, and covered it with lead; part of this he appropriated to the use of Goldsmith's work, and for other purposes relative to his Office; another Building taken notice of as built by him, was contiguous to the Infirmary; it was of stone, covered with lead, and had convenient offices under it, chiefly intended for the use of the *Custos* of the Infirmary. In his time also, Bells[13] were first put up in the great Western Tower."[14] Of this period the following are enumerated as works executed in the monastery[15]: Prior Crauden's chapel, the prior's new hall above the old one, the guest hall, the fair hall, and the residence of the sub-prior.

On the death of Bishop de Lisle in 1361, Walsingham was elected bishop by the convent, but the election was set aside by the pope. This eminent architect was buried in the cathedral, but the precise spot is not known. The epitaph on his tomb has been preserved, and in it we find that he was buried "ante Chorum" (in front of the choir). This would mean the ritual choir as then existing, and would fix the place of his interment approximately at the spot where there is now a large monumental slab, from which the brass has been removed; and this has always been traditionally said to be the actual stone placed over his body. The brass represented an ecclesiastic with mitre and pastoral staff. The objection to this having been Walsingham's memorial, that these emblems could not have been correctly placed upon it, has been thus met: "On the other hand it is contended that although Alan died a Prior of the Convent, he had been elected Bishop by the Monks, though his election was overruled by the Pope, and that seeing to his successor Prior Powcher

---

[13] The largest of these bells, weighing 6,280 pounds, was called by Walsingham's name.

[14] Bentham, pp. 221, 222.

[15] "Handbook," ed. Stubbs, 20th ed., p. 29.

the Pope gave permission that he and all future Priors of Ely should wear the mitre and carry the crozier, it is possible that the Monks had anticipated somewhat the Pope's edict, and had represented their beloved Prelate with episcopal mitre on his head and crozier in his hand."[16] He well deserved the description in the epitaph, "Flos operatorum" ("The Flower of Craftsmen"). The rich woodwork in the choir—the stalls with their beautiful canopies—is also certainly Walsingham's work.

Besides the great operations of this century there were various alterations and additions made in the cathedral of which the date is not recorded. The triforium in the presbytery was rearranged; the external walls were raised, and the Early English windows of Northwold's work were replaced by much larger ones with Decorated tracery. As the clerestory windows were not altered, the lean-to roof of the triforium was of course made much more flat than before. The graceful flying buttresses, with their elegant pinnacles, are of this same date. The character of Northwold's triforium windows and the corbel table below the parapet may be still seen in two bays on the south side. The aisle windows of the presbytery were also enlarged in the Decorated period; but they are not of the same design as the triforium windows, and they were probably not inserted at the same time. Judging by ordinary methods of discriminating dates by character and style, we should suppose the aisle windows to be earlier than those above; possibly some of this was done by Bishop Barnet (1366-1373). The whole designing is so unlike any of Walsingham's known work that we can hardly suppose that he was the author.

After the extensive changes of the fourteenth century were completed, the fabric of the cathedral was left practically as we see it now. Rearrangements of the interior have taken place on many occasions since, and the numerous side-chapels have been despoiled of their altars; but there has been no material structural change.

From the death of Bishop Barnet in 1373 to the suppression of the monasteries no Bishop of Ely is credited with having done anything towards the fabric of the cathedral except Bishop Gray (1454-1478). Some of them were at variance with the prior and convent, and would be little inclined to spend money on the church. Those that had a taste for architecture displayed it in beautifying their palaces or manor-houses, or upon buildings connected with the universities or other places in which they had private interest. Some were men of great political influence, and found their time and energies fully occupied in matters of national importance. One at least spent immense sums upon the drainage of the fens. Some did indeed erect chapels or shrines in the cathedral, or left provision that they should be erected after their deaths, but these were as memorials of themselves. The monastery carried out whatever was done in the fifteenth and sixteenth centuries as long as the monastery existed. The first such work was begun early in the fifteenth century by Prior Powcher: this was the erection of the upper portion of the western tower. At the top of the tower, before this addition, there was a wooden spire covered with lead. The upper story now is octagonal, and there are also octagonal turrets at the corners, detached, except at top and bottom, from the main body. These

---

[16] Ibid., p. 83. The full epitaph is given on p. 84.

were clearly built so as to harmonise with the large projecting turrets—massive enough themselves to be called towers—at the ends of the west front. This octagon was also itself—but probably at a much later date—surmounted with some sort of spire. An engraving dated 1786 shows this spire: it was no improvement to the tower. It was happily removed early in the nineteenth century. This additional story was built without due preparation. The extra weight was too much for the support which had been sufficient for the smaller tower; accordingly casing was added round the four great piers to increase the support. This was in Bishop Gray's time, and he contributed largely towards the cost. "The Prior and Convent were at great charges in repairing the lower part of the Western Tower; the Arches and Pillars of which, being found insufficient for its support, were therefore obliged to be strengthened, by wholly new-casing them with Stone, in the most substantial manner, as we now see them."[17] It has been reasonably conjectured that this extra weight was the cause of the ruin of the northern part of the west transept, or that it was then damaged beyond repair. To Bishop Gray is also assigned in particular the insertion of two windows in the north aisle of the presbytery, near the place where he was afterwards buried. The undoubted Decorated character of the upper stage of the west tower marks it as belonging to the very earliest years of the century. There is not the least tendency towards any features of the Perpendicular style. Without reckoning tombs and chapels, there is no structural work of distinct Perpendicular character to be seen at Ely Cathedral, except some remains of the cloisters, and the windows in the nave aisles and clerestory, and those in the upper parts of the great transept, and the large supporting arches which have been inserted beneath the Norman arches of the west tower. The triforium walls in the nave were raised in the fifteenth century, as those in the presbytery had been raised in the fourteenth. The style of the tracery shews that this alteration was carried out quite late in the century, perhaps about 1480. In the south transept there is also a large Perpendicular window. The very late east window of the south presbytery aisle was inserted as part of Bishop West's Chapel, who died in 1533.

In 1539 the monastery was surrendered to the king. Such of the domestic buildings as were not required for the use of the dean and canons were as usual sold. The Constitution of Henry VIII. provided for the customary officers of a cathedral establishment. The prior became the first dean, and remained in office till his death, eighteen years later. Though the minster had become a cathedral when the bishopric was instituted, yet the prior and convent were always custodians of the fabric, and apparently supreme therein; and there was nothing strictly corresponding to a capitular body. A memory of the fact that the bishop was in place of the abbot remains to this day in the position of the bishop's seat in the choir. There is no throne, properly so called. The bishop occupies what is in most cathedrals the dean's seat—on the south of the entrance at the screen. The north side is in consequence the Decani side, and the Cantoris side is on the south. This position of the dean's stall on the north, though very unusual, is not unique. It occurs also at Durham and Carlisle; but at those cathedrals there is a throne for the bishop, and the bishop's seat in a stall in the south, corresponding to the dean's in the <u>north, is not met</u> with elsewhere. "At Ely alone, of all cathedrals in Christendom,

[17] Bentham, pp. 177, 178.

owing to its first bishop having been an abbot who was himself the banished bishop of another see, the diocesan has continued to occupy the abbot's stall, while the head of the corporation (before the Reformation a prior, and since then a dean) has occupied the opposite stall, usually assigned to a sub-prior or sub-dean."[18] There were three Benedictine abbeys which retained their monastic establishment after a bishop had been made and the minster became a cathedral—Canterbury, Durham, and Ely.

It is always taken for granted that the destruction of the beautiful work in the lady-chapel, as well as of the shrines and statuary in the cathedral, was effected very soon after the dissolution of the monastery; but precise authority for this seems not to be forthcoming. It is known that Bishop Goodrich was an ardent supporter of the Reformation movement, and that he issued an injunction in 1541 which would have authorised such destruction. There was no other material damage done to the cathedral at this time. In 1566 a parish church, dedicated to S. Cross, which was situated at the north side of the nave, was found to be so dilapidated that no attempt was made to render it fit for service, and the dean and chapter gave to the parishioners the lady-chapel for a parish church, and it has so remained to this day.

It is probable that the wealth of the monastery had kept the fabric itself in such a state of complete repair that there was no occasion for much sustentation work for a long time after the Reformation—at least, we read nothing of any work being undertaken or of any portions of the building falling into decay. In the Commonwealth period the cathedral suffered less than in many places. The stained glass was indeed destroyed, and the cloisters and some parts of the domestic buildings pulled down, by order of commissioners. As Oliver Cromwell was Governor of the Isle of Ely, and often in the city, he was not likely to let the cathedral services alone. In January, 1644, he interfered during service, and stopped it, ejecting the congregation, and is said to have professed that this was an act of kindness, in order to prevent damage to the building. According to Carlyle,[19] he had written to the officiating minister, requiring him "to forbear altogether the choir service, so unedifying and offensive, lest the soldiers should in any tumultuary or disorderly way attempt the reformation of the cathedral church." If the people of Ely had heard about the "reformation" of the cathedral church at Peterborough, as carried out by the soldiers of the Parliament in July of the preceding year, they were certainly well advised in taking this hint. Bishop Wren—an eager opponent of the Puritans—was at the time in prison, where he remained until the Restoration.

The only account we have met with of disrepair in the seventeenth century says: "A little part of the end of the North Part fell down *March* 28, *Anno* 1699, but it was soon neatly rebuilt again at the Charge of the Church, with some Assistance from a Brief."[20] This was the north-west[21] corner of the north transept. The re-

---

[18] Hope's "The English Cathedral of the Nineteenth Century," p. 178.

[19] Quoted in Murray's "Handbook," p. 258.

[20] Browne Willis's "Survey," vol. iii., p. 334.

[21] Hewett ("Brief History," p. 24) says the north-eastern angle, and gives the date 1669; but the account in the text is correct.

building was carried out under the direction of Sir Christopher Wren, nephew of the bishop.

There is an account of the impression produced upon a visitor to Ely in the reign of William and Mary, the quaintness of which may perhaps justify the length of the quotation: "The Bishop does not care to stay long in this place, not being good for his health; he is Lord of all the island, has the command and ye jurisdiction.... There is a good palace for the Bishop built, but it was unfurnished. There are two Churches. Ely Minster is a curious pile of building all of stone, the outside full of Carvings and great arches, and fine pillars in the front, and the inside has the greatest variety and neatness in the works. There are two Chappels, most exactly carv'd in stone, all sorts of figures, Cherubims Gilt, and painted in some parts. Ye Roofe of one Chappell was One Entire stone most delicately Carv'd and hung down in great poynts all about ye Church. The pillars are Carv'd and painted with ye history of the bible, especially the new testament and description of Christ's miracles. The Lanthorn in ye quire are vastly high and delicately painted, and fine Carv'd work all of wood. In it ye bells used to be hung (five); the demention of ye biggest was so much that when they rung them it shooke ye quire so, and ye Carv'd worke, that it was thought unsafe; therefore they were taken down. There is one Chappel for Confession, with a Roome and Chaire of State for ye priest to set to hear ye people on their knees Confess into his Eare through a hole in ye wall. This Church has ye most popish remaines of any I have seen. There still remains a Cross over the alter; the Candlesticks are 3 quarters of a yard high, massy silver gilt, very heavy. The ffont is One Entire piece of White Marble, stemm and foote; the Cover was Carv'd Wood, with ye image of Christ's being baptised by John, and the holy Dove descending on him, all finely Carv'd white wood, without any paint or varnish."[22]

In the eighteenth century some extensive repairs became necessary, and some alterations in the arrangements of the choir were carried out. The former chiefly affected the roofs of the octagon and presbytery. Other parts of the cathedral seem to have needed some repair, but not to a considerable extent. The latter consisted in the moving of the ritual choir to the extreme east end of the church, the returned stalls at its western limit being at the sixth piers from the east end. This alteration was effected in 1770.

The position of the high altar has been perhaps more often moved in this cathedral than in any other. In the Norman choir the altar was situated in the centre of the fourth bay east of the present octagon. When Bishop Northwold enlarged the presbytery it was moved one bay further east. After the rebuilding of the three bays west of Northwold's work, it seems to have been moved again westward, as far as the first piers east of the octagon. Again in 1770, at the time of which we are now speaking, it was moved to the extreme east end, and was placed just against the east wall. Now it stands between the second piers from the east.

It is not a little singular to notice the enthusiasm with which this eigh-

[22] "Through England On a Side-Saddle in the time of William and Mary, being the Diary of Celia Fiennes." Published 1888. Quoted in "Fenland Notes and Queries," vol. i., pp. 291-293.

teenth-century change was greeted. Bentham says[23] it was "an alteration which had long been wished for, by all persons of true taste." And again: "It is allowed by the best judges to be one of the most useful and ornamental Improvements that could have been effected"; and he gives a long disquisition highly praising the alteration. The eastern portion, formerly "an useless encumbrance," was now brought into use. The organ and voices could be better heard, the view of the octagon was greatly improved, and the nave and transepts "have acquired their due Dimensions." Compare this with Hewett's observations less than eighty years later: "Never was there a more ill-judged step than the removal of the Choir hither, towards the latter portion of the last century. To give it such stinted proportions, and for this purpose to displace some of the fine old monuments, and to hide others, to obscure the pillars, and, above all, to erect the miserable organ gallery which we now behold, may surely be pronounced most tasteless performances"[24] When he wrote, the proposal was to replace Walsingham's stalls in the octagon, and to make Bishop Hotham's three Decorated bays into a sacrarium, and so presumably re-erect the high altar on the very spot where it stood in Norman times.

Bishop Mawson contributed £1000 towards the removal of the choir to the east end. He had also been at the expense of paving the choir with black and white marble, and of inserting stained glass at the east end. The work done at this time was under the superintendence of the architect Essex. An organ-gallery was placed at the entrance of the choir: judging by the plan given by Bentham, this occupied the whole of the eastern bay of Hotham's work. Screens of some sort are marked as crossing both aisles, as a continuation of the western face of this organ-gallery: or perhaps these were only metal gates. The design of the whole seems to have been very poor: "the miserable organ gallery" is what Hewett calls it. The original stone screen that formed the entrance to the choir before the tower fell, situated in the bay of the nave next to the octagon, was still standing. It had served as the organ-loft until the alteration. Browne Willis, who wrote before Bishop Mawson came to Ely, records that the choir had been paved with black and white marble at the charge of Bishop Gunning, and that he had proposed to move the choir to the east end nearly a hundred years before it was actually done, "which if he had done ... it would have added vastly to the Beauty of the Church."[25]

Still later in the century, in 1796, Wyatt "the destructive" was directed to make a report on the state of the fabric, and to supply estimates for a restoration. Among other things he recommended the selling of the lead on the roof, the removal of the rood-loft, and the reducing of the number of bells from five to one.

---

[23] Page 214.
[24] Page 17.
[25] Page 334.

ELY CATHEDRAL AT THE END OF THE EIGHTEENTH CENTURY.

From Stevenson's Supplement to Bentham.

The nineteenth century began with works of destruction. In 1801[26] the spire on the tower was taken down. Soon afterwards, in accordance with Wyatt's recommendation, the ancient rood-loft in the nave was removed. As it had ceased to be

[26] Date so given in "Handbook," 20th ed.

the entrance to the choir, it was probably deemed useless. The roof of the galilee was also removed, and the lancets at the west of the cathedral blocked up. Mr. Bernasconi's contract, in 1801, for the repair of part of the west end, amounting to £232 14s. 6d.,[27] probably covered the whole of this. A note on the receipt speaks of a picture at the east end in 1800, a pulpit in 1806, and a new window in 1808; but whether all these were new or merely repaired does not appear. From Goodwin's "Ely Gossip" we learn that the upper part of the doorway of the galilee porch was "renewed in plaster." In a pamphlet published in 1827 it is said that "so much has been done to this cathedral of late as to afford a reasonable ground of hope, that ere long the beautiful Purbeck shafts will be cleared of the yellow ochre which coats and defiles them, and that the earth will be cleared away from the walls on the north side, where at present it is injuring both walls and pavement."[28] What had then been recently done, and thus mentioned, apparently with approval, did not long satisfy the public taste, although a large outlay testified to the good intentions, if not the judgment, of the authorities. Walsingham's stalls were painted; and the nave, octagon, lantern, and transepts were colour-washed. Within about twenty-five years what had been introduced as embellishments were removed as disfigurements, and the removal cost possibly as much as the introduction.

Soon after Dean Peacock came to Ely he commenced the restoration and decoration of the fabric which have gone on continuously to the present time, and are not yet complete. Besides many munificent gifts, of which the cost is not known, upwards of £70,000 has been expended upon the works at the cathedral since 1843. The first great work included in this sum was the entire re-leading of the roof. In 1842 there had been a fire discovered in the roof near the west tower, but no great damage was done. Most likely it was the prospect of having to spend large sums upon the cathedral itself that induced the dean and chapter to sanction the demolition of the sextry-barn, "on the ground that the repairs it required were too expensive." This barn was situated to the north of the lady-chapel. It was an object of the greatest architectural interest, and its destruction is much to be lamented. It was of Early English date, and is said to have been a "noble and almost unrivalled" building. It seems to have been of the same character as the abbey tithe-barn at Peterborough, which was perfect a very few years ago, and of which the whole of the wooden posts and beams are still to be seen *in situ*. The Peterborough barn was also of thirteenth century date; it had aisles and nave all formed by the oak beams and supports. The Ely barn was much smaller.

In July, 1845, the restoration had been well begun, and was being carried on with energy. The works in Bishop Alcock's chapel had been commenced. The south end of the west transept, hitherto used as a kind of storehouse or lumber-room, was repaired and thrown open to the church. A poor deal roof was added as a temporary protection. The choir roof was scraped and cleaned. In the lady-chapel the colour-wash that had obscured the remains of the beautiful carvings was removed. The west tower was ceiled. Up to this time there appears to have been no properly qualified architect in charge of the work. In 1847 Mr. Scott (afterwards Sir

---

[27] Gibbons' "Ely Episcopal Records," p. 112.
[28] "Notes on the Cambridgeshire Churches," p. 4.

G. G. Scott) was appointed architect to the cathedral. He soon made an extensive examination of the whole building, and issued a report upon the state of the fabric and the amount of restoration needful.

Dean Peacock, who so thoroughly identified himself with the restoration, died in 1858. His successor, Dean Goodwin, entered with enthusiasm upon the work, and was instrumental in raising large sums of money for the carrying out of the architect's designs. After he had been dean seven years he published a paper upon the progress that had been made, which commences with these words: "The time seems to be now come, when the completion of the great work of restoration, commenced under Dean Peacock, and guided for many years by his care and judgment, may be looked upon as within reach."[29] In this paper he enumerated these works as already accomplished:

1. The choir restored and rearranged.
2. Central lantern restored (Peacock Memorial).
3. South-east transept restored.
4. South-west transept restored.
5. Roof of north transept restored and painted.
6. Nave ceiled and painted.
7. Nave roof repaired and re-leaded.
8. S. Catherine's chapel rebuilt.
9. Bishop Alcock's chapel restored.
10. Galilee porch re-paved.
11. Western tower opened, ceiled, re-roofed, strengthened, etc.
12. About seventy windows filled with stained glass.

Of the painting the north transept roof the expense was borne by the tradesmen employed upon the cathedral. The restoration of Bishop Alcock's chapel was undertaken, out of respect to the memory of their founder, by Jesus College, Cambridge. The painting of the nave ceiling was the work of Mr. le Strange and Mr. Gambier Parry, the former of whom also painted the ceiling of the west tower. Exclusive of special donations for specific works included in the above list, the dean reckoned that up to the time of his report £27,185 had been spent, of which the dean and chapter had contributed no less than £15,200. Several individual members of the chapter had, besides money gifts, presented windows or other decorations, or had been responsible for various structural repairs. At a rough estimate the total sum expended had amounted to £40,000. The works still to be executed were these:

1. Paving the nave, octagon, and transepts.
2. Completion of pinnacles and parapet of octagon.
3. Internal decoration of lantern.
4. Repair of galilee.

There would also be much to be done in the matter of properly warming and lighting the cathedral; but those expenses were more strictly within the ordinary obligations of the dean and chapter.

[29] "Ecclesiologist," xxvii., p. 71.

The only one of the above works that calls for special notice is the restoration of the octagon and lantern. In a statement circulated by the dean and chapter in 1853 it was declared that "of all works which remain to be undertaken, the most considerable and the most important is the restoration of the lantern, including the decoration of the vault, the substitution of windows of an appropriate character for those which now disfigure it so seriously, and the addition of the outer corona of turrets and pinnacles as originally designed by Alan de Walsingham." But nothing was done towards this during Dean Peacock's lifetime. In the summer before his death he had described more particularly the disfigurements and the mutilations which the lantern had undergone; and he further pointed out the unsafe condition of the exterior. The upper windows of the octagon were of the "meanest description of carpenter's Gothic"; they had been reduced from four to three lights each; they had been shortened more than three feet (probably by Essex in the eighteenth century); the upper timbers were in a ruinous state, and incapable of being used again. The original design provided for eight lofty turrets at the angles of the greater octagon and four pinnacles in the middle of its longer sides. At the first meeting of the chapter after Dean Peacock's death it was resolved that no memorial of him would be so appropriate as the restoration of the lantern, and Mr. Scott was instructed to prepare designs at once. A tentative sketch of his design was published in October, 1859; and the opinion of experts was invited. Mr. Scott's report, dated June 10, 1859, gave the result of his careful examination. He concluded that the wooden lantern was originally "to a certain extent an imitation of the general form of the *stone octagon* below it. Each had large windows of four lights below, with circular panels in the spandrils; each had a distinct story over these windows, lighted by smaller windows consisting of several detached lights, and each had considerable turrets, probably surmounted by pinnacles at the angles, and, in all probability, open parapets between them."[30] He embodied the results of the evidence he had got together in the design he submitted. Further examination, in the following year, satisfied the architect that no spire had ever been erected on the lantern, and that even if Walsingham had ever intended to have one, he had yet finished his work without any preparation for such an addition. A design for such a spire was, however, prepared and submitted to the dean and chapter, but it was never adopted.

As was to be expected, many opinions were expressed upon the design. Some wanted the whole to be surmounted by a pyramidal capping. It was objected that the design was a stone construction for what must of necessity be erected of wood. It was pointed out that Walsingham used his upper story as a bell-chamber, and argued that a true restoration should aim at reproducing this feature. In the end Scott's design was carried out exactly as proposed, except that the eight small square turrets of the wooden lantern have no pinnacles.

The enumeration of works completed in 1866, as given by Dean Goodwin above, did not include several important and costly gifts. The chief of these were: the carved panels above the stalls, supplied by individual donors; a pinnacle at the south-east corner of the choir (Mr. Beresford Hope); the reredos (Mr. J. Dunn

---

[30] "Ecclesiologist," xxi., p. 26.

Gardner); the font (Canon Selwyn); the gates of aisles of presbytery (Mr. Lowndes and Dean Peacock); the brass eagle lectern (Canon E. B. Sparke); and the monumental effigies of Bishop Allen and Dr. Mill. Canon E. B. Sparke had also contributed to the restoration of the south transept; Mr. H. R. Evans, sen., and Mr. H. R. Evans, jun., had helped with the works in the west tower; the Rev. G. Millers, minor canon, had bequeathed £100, and his residuary legatees gave another £300, which was applied to the ceiling of the nave; Miss Allen, daughter of the bishop, also bequeathed £500, appropriated to a new pulpit; and Bishop Turton left the same amount for re-paving the nave.

The only other work of importance done before Dean Goodwin left for Carlisle was the reconstruction of the organ. Canon Dickson, in his admirable historical account of the organ, is confident that the instrument in use in 1831 was the original pre-Reformation organ, gradually enlarged from time to time with "all the improvements suggested by the progress of musical and mechanical art." Its preservation during the Commonwealth period is possibly due to the personal influence of Oliver Cromwell. About that date (1831) the organ was rebuilt by Elliott and Hill. It was fitted into the old cases, of Renaissance design. From the similarity of these cases to some which are known to have inclosed organs built by Renatus Harris, the old organ has sometimes been attributed to him; but there is "no record whatever of the employment of Harris by the Dean and Chapter."

The progress made in the time of Dean Merivale (1869-1894) was steady and substantial, but calls for no detailed account. The foundations of many parts of the building were made more secure; much of the pavement was renewed; the tower at the west was strengthened with iron bands; several stained glass windows were inserted. Perhaps the most noteworthy undertaking of this period was the decoration of the interior, and the completion of the series of pinnacles of the exterior, of the octagon and lantern. In a summary of the amount spent between 1843 and 1898 the total, exclusive of special gifts, is given at £69,543 1s. 0d.[31]

---

[31] "Handbook," 20th ed., App. II.

THE CATHEDRAL FROM THE WEST.

ENTRANCE TO THE CATHEDRAL FROM THE GALILEE.

CHAPTER II.

THE CATHEDRAL: EXTERIOR.

Few persons would dispute the statement that for external grandeur of effect the cathedral at Ely is surpassed only, if at all, in England by Durham and Lincoln. With the natural advantages of position enjoyed by those cathedrals Ely cannot compete. In both these cases, also, there are grand mediæval buildings of great size near at hand, that group well with the cathedrals and materially improve the effect. But, compared with the adjacent country, Ely does stand on an eminence, and consequently can be seen from a great distance in all directions. At Durham the distant view is limited by the hilly nature of the district; Lincoln, except on the north side, can probably be seen more than thirty miles off, from the ground.[32] Ely can be seen quite well from the tower of Peterborough—about thirty-five miles as the crow flies. Ely is nearly, but not quite, the highest spot in the Fenland. One place in Ely is 109 feet above mean sea-level. The highest elevation in the Fenland is near Haddenham, some five miles to the south-west of Ely, where a few bench-marks give 121 and 122 feet above sea-level.

[32] Not many persons who travel by the Great Northern main line know that a good view of Lincoln Cathedral is to be obtained from it.

It is not only its magnificence that makes the view of Ely Cathedral so remarkable, there is also the feeling that it has so many striking features, to which we can find nothing to compare. "The first glimpse of Ely overwhelms us, not only by its stateliness and variety of its outline, but by its utter strangeness, its unlikeness to anything else." So says Professor Freeman[33] and again: "Ely, ... with its vast single western tower, with its central octagon unlike anything else in the whole world, has an outline altogether peculiar to itself."

Although Ely, with the single exception of Wells,[34] is the smallest of the ancient episcopal cities[35] of England, the area of the cathedral is exceeded only by four others—York, S. Paul's, Lincoln, and Winchester. The church certainly gives the impression of being out of all proportion to the town.[36] There has been nothing to occasion any considerable increase in the number of the inhabitants. Sixty years ago there were within about four hundred as many as now. The town, as has been pointed out above, grew out of the foundation of the monastery. "The history of Ely is the history of Wells, Lichfield, Peterborough, Bury Saint Edmunds, and a crowd of others, where the church came first and the town grew up at the gate of the bishop or abbot." The great wealth of the monastery accounts for the original magnificence of the church; and even when the resources both of the see and the cathedral body were reduced, they were still amply sufficient to maintain the fabric without the loss of any material portion of it. We have no knowledge of the occasion of the ruin of the northern part of the west transept, but there is no suggestion that it was allowed to fall through want of means to keep it up.

THE WEST FRONT

The West Front.—The visitor will naturally commence his investigation of the cathedral with studying the view of the tower from the west; and here he should endeavour to picture to himself the appearance of the west front as it originally stood. It has, indeed, been questioned whether the northern limb of the western transept had ever been really completed. The prevailing opinion is that it was completed, and the weather-mould against the north wall of the tower is held by many to be almost conclusive evidence of the fact. From what we see remaining, it is clear that it was (if ever built) similar to the southern limb; and it was doubtless terminated in the same way by two massive octangular towers. Imagine, therefore, a west front, having to the left of the tower (as we look at it from the west) a limb corresponding to that on the right; imagine also a line of roof, extending over both western transepts, situated in a line with the foot of the three lancet windows

---

[33] Introduction to Farren's "Cathedral Cities of Ely and Norwich."

[34] Population of Ely, 1891, was 6,646; of Wells, 5,899.

[35] Ely is almost universally called a city, upon the supposition that the mere fact of its having a cathedral constitutes the town a city. But since the Norman Conquest the dignity of a city has always been conferred by grant, and no such grant is known to have been made to Ely.

[36] An American visitor whom the writer was once conducting over Peterborough Cathedral observed, "This is a very large church for so small a place." Ely is about a quarter of the size of Peterborough in respect to population.

just below the clock; imagine also, further, a roof of similar pitch over the galilee porch,[37] and, instead of the present Decorated stage at the summit, a pyramidal spire of timber, leaded. "The front, with its tower thus terminated, with leaded spires also on the four terminal towers of the transept, and with the high roofs of the transept and western porch, must have presented a _tout ensemble_ of the most imposing and majestic character."[38]

When we examine the details of the architecture we can express nothing but the greatest admiration. The whole of the south wing of the front belongs to the last quarter of the twelfth century. The lowest stage of all (for there are six stages, divided by horizontal strings) is blank; the next three are late Norman. These have in the lowest stage in each of the two divisions an arcade of seven tall lancets; in the next above are four broader arches, each containing two small lancets beneath; in the upper one is a large window, under a round arch of four receding orders, with a blank lancet on each side. In the north wing, it should be noted, the late Norman work was carried up one stage higher than on the south. The upper stages are Transitional in character, but they carry on the idea of the Norman design below. Here we see first an arcade of four trefoiled lancets, of greater depth than those underneath; while the uppermost stage has a large pointed window, with a lancet on each side, and above each lancet a quatrefoil in a circle. The arches of the window and lancets are highly enriched with carving. Below the parapet is a good corbel table. The fourth and sixth stages are further covered with admirable diaper panel-work. The octagonal towers at the end of the southern transept, of which that to the west is larger than the other, have three more stages, the central one having small, deeply sunk trefoiled lancets; the other two, large plain ones; the uppermost tier of lancets being open. A singular effect is produced in the third stage from the top by the lancets being divided in the centre by the main shaft that rises from the ground at the angles of the tower. On the south and east these shafts are not perfect.

THE GALILEE PORCH

The Galilee Porch is of excellent Early English work, with details of great beauty. Certainly nowhere in England, possibly nowhere in the world, is there to be seen so fine a porch. "Perhaps the most gorgeous porch of this style in existence is the Galilee at the west end of Ely Cathedral: this magnificent specimen of the Early English style must be seen to be duly appreciated; it combines the most elegant general forms with the richest detail; a very happy effect is produced by the double arcade on each side, one in front of the other with detached shafts, not opposite but alternate."[39] Each side, externally, is covered with lancet arcading in four tiers. In the upper tier the lancets are trefoiled, with dogtooth in the moulding; in the next lower tier the lancets are cinquefoiled, with two sets of dogtooth.

---

[37] But there is no indication that such a roof actually reached the tower.

[38] Scott's Paper, read at Bissexcentenary Festival, 1873.

[39] From the additions to Rickman's "Attempt to Discriminate the Styles of Architecture in England," given in the 5th ed., 1848. The "happy effect" described is in the interior of the porch.

The lancets in the west face are all cinquefoiled, and the three lower tiers here have trefoils in the spandrels. Nearly all are highly enriched with dogtooth; while the mouldings of the west door have conventional foliage as well. The lancets here are deeper than on the sides of the porch, and were probably designed to hold figures. Of the three large lancets in the west window the central one is slightly more lofty than the others.

DOORWAY OF THE GALILEE.

The interior of the porch is even more beautiful; the profusion of ornamentation on the inner doorway and the exceeding gracefulness of the double arcades in the sides are quite unsurpassed. Both doorways are divided by a shaft, and both have open tracery of exceptional beauty above.

Bishop Eustace, to whom this porch is attributed, died in 1215. It is not surprising to learn that many careful students of English architecture have found a difficulty in believing that work of such consummate grace and perfection of detail can belong to so early a date. Many dated examples belonging to later years in the century, which seem to indicate a steady growth from the simplest pointed lancets to the elaborately cusped arches which were themselves the prelude to the Geometric period, are adduced as evidence of the improbability of the Early English style having, so to say, grown suddenly to perfection at Ely. Numerous instances may, however, be found in other great minsters, where a similar difficulty has been encountered. The probable explanation is that the best artists and the most original designers belonged to the monastic or cathedral bodies. They maintained what would be described in modern language as schools of architects; and the very best talents and energies of such bodies would naturally be brought to bear upon any great work connected with their own church. We cannot suppose that a new conception in architectural design sprang into existence simultaneously in several different centres. There must have been a beginning in some one place. The idea would spread in the neighbourhood and in buildings where the particular abbey or cathedral had property or influence, and would by degrees be carried to other religious houses, and so become generally adopted, and mark a distinct change in style. But this would take time. Sometimes we can trace how new methods were carried about. Those who were brought over from Normandy by the Norman kings of England to be abbots in English monasteries, brought with them their characteristic style of building; and at the end of the twelfth century this had entirely superseded the old English style. One monastery passed on the new fashion to another, as Simeon, at Ely, came fresh from the great work being carried on at Winchester under his brother Walkelin.

It is not claimed for Bishop Eustace that his work here is the earliest known specimen of the style finished in so perfect a form. At Lincoln the choir was erected in the time of Bishop Hugh, who died in 1200. Some features there have been pointed out that shew that the style was a new departure, and that the architect was feeling his way. It is admitted that there is not to be found an earlier dated example of the finest Early English work than the choir at Lincoln. Second only to this the galilee porch at Ely may take rank. Other erections of very nearly the same date have admirable work, such as the lady-chapel at Winchester and the east end of Chichester; but there is nothing in either of those examples to compare with the elaborate richness of detail at Ely.

THE WEST TOWER

The West Tower has six stages of Early English date above the porch. Three of these have each three separate lancet windows, the two lower having banded shafts. In the projecting corner turrets are lancets of similar design in the two upper stages, but not so broad and not pierced for windows; while in the lowest stage in the turrets above the porch are several tall, thin, trefoiled lancets, having more the character of Transition Norman work. Between the window ranges are arcades of short, deep, trefoiled lancets; at the top below the parapet and corbel table are five quatrefoils in circles, one not pierced. On the north and south sides are but two ranges of windows. The tower must, of course, have been built before the porch, and may consequently be assigned to the last years of the twelfth century; and it is a noble specimen for such an early date. The upper Decorated stage consists of an octagon having a fine window of three lights in each face, the part below the transom not glazed, and an open parapet above. At the corners are octagonal turrets, with open lights above the level of the central portion, and plain parapets. The turrets are detached from the centre, except at the top and bottom. The latest calculations give the height of these turrets as 215 feet. This would be nearly the same as the central tower at Durham.

The Early English tower must have had some erection above it, probably of wood, of a low pyramidal form. But before long it was replaced by something of a better style. Bishop Northwold (1229-1254) "construxit de novo turrim ligneam versus galileam ab opere cementario usque ad summitatem." This was in turn removed when the present octagonal stage was erected, about the year 1400. This addition was soon found to be a source of danger, and it threatened the destruction of the whole tower. For several years, in the middle of the fifteenth century, the tower was undergoing repairs. Before this the upper part had been braced together with frames of timber. In the interior, as will be seen hereafter, inner arches of great strength were inserted under the original Norman arches of the tower. A light and thin wooden spire was unwisely placed at the top, and this was in 1757 reported to be in bad condition, and injurious to the tower. It was not finally restored till about 1801, when the whole of the upper portion, including the corner turrets, was materially strengthened.

On the west face of the buttress, built against the tower in the north, can be seen some panels of Perpendicular date. These have suggested the idea that it was in contemplation to rebuild what had fallen in a later style.

THE WEST TOWER FROM THE SOUTH.

Photochrom Co. Ltd.

THE NORTH SIDE OF THE NAVE

Notwithstanding the ruins, the view of the cathedral from the north-west is very striking, and in some respects more remarkable than any other (see p. 2). We have here the only external view of the whole length of the **North Side Of**

The Nave. With the exception of the clerestory range, and, of course, the north transept, the first impression is not that of a Norman building. The single broad light of the Norman clerestory, with its adjacent round-headed lancets in the wall, remains in each bay unaltered. Above these windows was once a battlement; but Miller records, in 1834, that it was "removed within the last sixty years." The aisle battlement remains. The walls of the triforium were raised, and the Norman windows, both of the aisle and triforium, altered, in the Perpendicular period, the alterations having been begun on the south side in 1469. All these windows now have ogee arches, and are of three lights. The tracery is unimposing. About the middle of the wall can be distinctly seen the marks of the door and covered way that led from the cathedral to the Church of S. Cross. This church had been erected in the early part of the fourteenth century, but (as has been mentioned, p. 29), was found in 1566 to be too dilapidated for use, and beyond repair. It was accordingly destroyed, and the lady-chapel assigned, in lieu of it, to the parishioners for their parish church. Either the fabric of this church must have been strangely neglected by its custodians, or it must have been very inferior in merit of construction to Walsingham's work, which was being erected at the same time, if it could last no longer than about two hundred and thirty years. Round the clerestory windows and arcading can be seen the billet moulding; under the triforium parapet is a corbel table with billets; below the triforium windows is a string-course consisting of little double squares with a diagonal (sometimes called the hatched moulding), a form of ornament not one of the most common. Good examples of it are to be seen in Westminster Hall. In the sixth bay from the transept is a tablet with the date 1662. This must be the time when some alterations were made; but it can neither refer to the raising of the triforium walls, nor to the building up the wall when the door to the destroyed church was no longer needed. Between this point and the transepts can be plainly seen the marks of the original Norman windows over the heads of the existing Perpendicular ones.

THE OCTAGON

The Octagon can be nowhere seen to better advantage than from this point of view. Restored as a memorial to Dean Peacock, it has been brought as nearly as possible to what Walsingham intended; for it is not quite certain that he entirely completed his own design. The quadrangular turrets, for instance, at the corners of the lantern, were probably meant to be surmounted by pinnacles. These were included in Scott's original designs for the restoration, but have not been erected. Indeed, two of Bentham's views of the building represent pinnacles at the corners of both octagon and lantern, while one view has them to neither. It is certain also that there were slighter pinnacles designed for the middle of the longer sides of the octagon. These have now been built. The lantern has quite recovered its original beauty, after being sadly mutilated and altered at various times. During the discussions about the correct way of completing the lantern not a few persons maintained that the true termination of the whole was a lofty, light, open spire, and that if Walsingham never erected one, he must, at least, have had one in contemplation. The examination of the interior construction leaves no doubt whatever that no such flèche was ever erected, and also that Walsingham intentionally completed the whole without making any preparation for the addition of such a feature, a preparation which he would beyond question have made had he thought a spire was necessary to the completion of the work.

The octagon is not equilateral. The cardinal faces, being equal to the inner breadth of the nave and transepts, are the longer. In all the faces just below the open parapet are arcades of cinquefoiled arches, some of them pierced for windows. The cardinal faces have each six such arches, and the other faces only three. These shorter sides only have large windows, the others abutting directly upon the roofs. These large windows have exquisite tracery; they are all of four lights, with transoms, and are beneath arches unusually acute for the Decorated period. The windows in the lantern are new, Essex having destroyed the original four-light windows and substituted poor ones of three lights each.

The way in which the octagon and lantern combine in producing a perfectly harmonious composition is in great part due to two points of difference, points which very few observers detect. These are, firstly, that the lantern is a regular octagon, having all its sides equal, in this respect being unlike the stone octagon beneath it; and, secondly, that the eight faces of the lantern are not parallel to the eight faces of the octagon. The new windows of the lantern are similar to the large ones below, but are not mere copies of them. The upper stage of the lantern, above the roof as seen from within, was once a bell-chamber; its lights are not, and never have been, glazed. The whole of the lantern is of wood, covered with lead. Two flying buttresses rise from the corners of the nave and transept aisles to the corbel table of the clerestory range. There are also eight elegant flying buttresses, one to each of the angles of the lantern. These are part of the new work, the originals having long disappeared.

THE NORTH TRANSEPT

The North Transept retains its original Norman windows in the lower stage of its western aisle, though we must remember that the north-western angle of this transept fell down in 1699, and was rebuilt[40] under the superintendence of Sir Christopher Wren. It is said that an earthquake had occurred some few years before, and had caused some damage which was not suspected at the time. However much we may admire Wren's constructive genius, we cannot justify the incongruous door in the north wall of the transept, for which we take it for granted he was responsible. It is in the classical style, utterly out of keeping with the architecture near. The arch and jambs of the Norman window above it were replaced; but this again is spoilt by the insertion of rude unadorned mullions. The corresponding window over the eastern aisle is original and unaltered. The north end of the transept has also Norman lights, larger than those below, on the second range; while above are two large Perpendicular windows, each of three lights, with transoms.

---

[40] Some money was raised towards the expense of this rebuilding by means of a brief. At Castor, co. Northants, 5s. 4½d. was sent "for Ely Cathedral"; this was in 1701. In the same year, at Bishop's Hatfield, co. Herts, £1 5s. 2½d. was raised upon the "Brief for Ely Cathedral." In the following year a brief was issued for a fire in the city of Ely, but it does not appear that this had anything to do with the cathedral.

To see the east wall of the transept we have to go round the lady-chapel. Here both triforium and clerestory are in their original Norman condition. The lower windows are Decorated.

THE LADY-CHAPEL

It cannot but be regretted that the two large windows east and west of **The Lady-Chapel** are not portions of the building as it stood at first. That to the east, of seven lights, is known to have been inserted by Bishop Barnet, who died in 1373. The authority for this is the sacrist's roll for that year. The item is given in Dean Stubbs' "Historical Memorials," p. 147. The bishop's executors paid £20 "for making a certain window in the lady-chapel near the high altar in the preceding year." The west window, of eight lights, is of somewhat later date. Considering that the chapel was finished in 1349, and that there is no reason to doubt that the east and west ends were adorned with fine windows of the same character as those in the sides, it seems extraordinary that within twenty-five years it should have been thought worth while to alter the eastern end. Was the alteration made in connection with the insertion of a grander reredos than had been at first provided? This seems possible, as may be judged from the following observations of the present Dean: "It is evident from indications supplied by the masonry of the central light of the east window, the mullions of which are of unusual solidity, that the Reredos and East window were originally combined in some structure, of which the chief object was the large figure of S. Mary, often mentioned in the Rolls of the Custos Capellæ, and which must have occupied a canopied niche, blocking up the whole of the middle light from sill to transom."[41] The design of the east window is inelegant, the transom is heavy, and the tracery in the large circle at the top spoils the effect of the window as a whole.

The west window, except for the central portion at the top and the heavy mullions, is just like two of the side windows placed side by side. But here again the vertical lines in the upper part harmonise ill with the rest. There are some good niches at the west end above the window, but there are no figures in them; and there are shallow arches on the surface of the wall, on each side of the window as well as beneath it. Above most of the niches are shields with heraldic bearings, twelve in all. Among these are the coats of Edward the Confessor, the See of Ely, Bishops Hotham, Montacute, Fordham, and perhaps Barnet.[42] One shield has a cross, and one a lion between three helmets. The arms of the monastery—three keys (said to have been adopted from Bishop Ethelwold of Winchester)—occur four times, in three cases with initials beneath. These initials are: A. W., which may certainly be assigned to Alan de Walsingham; J. C.; and C. W. S. From the occurrence of Bishop Fordham's arms we may conclude that this west end was reconstructed, or at least that its reconstruction was completed, in his time (1388-1425). In some of the lower niches are memorial tablets.

---

[41] "Historical Memorials," p. 116.

[42] One shield has a saltire: Bishop Barnet used a saltire with a leopard's head in chief.

THE CHOIR AND LADY-CHAPEL FROM THE NORTH-EAST.

On each side of the lady-chapel are five large windows of four lights each, with very beautiful tracery. Those on the north side have been thoroughly restored within the last few years. At the same time the cusps have been replaced in the large circles, of which two are over the head of each window. Between the windows are buttresses, necessarily large, to support the vast extent of the stone-groined roof. At the four corners are double buttresses, with much larger pinnacles, and two niches toward the top, the upper one shallow, but the lower deep enough to hold a statue, and with a projecting canopy. The east end is less decorated than the west. There was once, as it seems, some sculptured figure or figures in front of the upper part of the window, no doubt destroyed when the interior was mutilated.

ELEVATION OF ORIGINAL BAYS OF BISHOP NORTHWOLD'S PRESBY-
TERY.

THE EAST END

"The **East End** of the cathedral itself (Bishop Hugh's work) is a grand example of Early English."[43] Except for the windows of the chapels of Bishops Alcock and West in the aisles, and that the Early English lancets in the triforium range in the south aisle have been removed and a plain wall substituted, this eastern front is almost unaltered. It does not appear when this last alteration was made. In the view in Bentham, dated 1767, are represented lancets glazed and blank, exactly similar to those in the triforium on the north. The windows are all lancets, without any cusping. Their grouping is specially effective. In the centre, in the lowest stage, are three broad lancets of equal height, divided by shafts, and with deep mouldings, and with two sets of dogtooth all round. Below the string-course above are four deep quatrefoils. In the next stage the lancets are five in number, the central one being the tallest, while above the outer ones are trefoiled niches; and there are two six-foils below the next string-course. The upper stage has three lancets of equal height, which give light to the space above the stone-groined roof, with a small trefoiled arch, unglazed, and half of another on each side. In the gable are three large sunk panels, two of six cusps, and one of eight. The whole is surmounted by a large handsome cross, restored at the expense of Lady Mildred Hope. The large buttresses on each side of the central group of windows have four niches on each side, the three upper ones having bases to support statues; the upper and lower of these have trefoiled heads, the two others cinquefoiled heads. At the summit are sunk trefoils under the gabled tops; and a little further to the west, on the south, the whole is finished by an octangular turret with shallow arches and a pyramidal top with crockets.[44] The buttresses at the corners of the aisles have much loftier pyramidal heads. These have also crockets. The east end of the triforium range on the north is particularly good. The east window of Bishop Alcock's chapel, which was of course in existence long before his time, is round-headed, with four lights, and some good Decorated tracery. That to Bishop West's chapel, in the south aisle, is of five lights, of very late Perpendicular character. It may be noticed that the window in the north aisle is in the wall as originally built, but in the south aisle the whole wall has been advanced further east, as far as the bases of the buttresses.

THE AISLES

Both of **The Aisles** have on the sides large pinnacled buttresses of graceful design; and from all of these on the north, and from some on the south, there rise flying buttresses to support the roof of the presbytery and choir. Two of the bays on the south side have the Early English triforium range unaltered. This gives the original height of Bishop Hugh's triforium walls. Below the parapet here is a characteristic corbel table. These bays form the western portion of Bishop Hugh's work in the presbytery.

---

[43] Murray's "Eastern Cathedrals," p. 221.

[44] The cost of this pinnacle was defrayed by Mr. Beresford Hope. The corresponding pinnacle on the north is still wanting. It is, however, figured, by mistake, in the view of the east end in Murray's "Eastern Cathedrals."

THE LANTERN AND SOUTH TRANSEPT.

Photochrom Co. Ltd. Photo.

THE TRIFORIUM WINDOWS

The retention of this little portion of the Early English **Triforium** is very interesting and instructive; for we should otherwise not have known precisely how this part of the work had been carried out. Professor Willis traced out with great care the alterations to which the presbytery had been subjected, and his conclusions are given in Canon Stewart's book. Early triforium windows were only for lighting the triforium passage; they were small, and could not be seen from the floor of the church. It will be noticed that the windows remaining in the portion spoken of are quite small and quite close to the floor. The changes that were made in the three great Norman minsters, Norwich, Peterborough, and Ely, were "made evidently for the purpose of introducing more light into the church." The walls were raised, the windows much enlarged, and the slope of the roof consequently much flattened. No doubt, as regards dimensions, Bishop Hugh's triforium was a continuation of the Norman triforium of the choir. The first appearance of a high triforium outer wall is in Bishop Hotham's work (1316-1337). "In the following centuries this new form was extended by alterations, first to Hugh de Northwold's presbytery and next to the nave. But before the Early English gallery had been thus completely transformed, it happened that some architect, apparently employed by Bishop Barnet (1366-1374), introduced in two of the southern compartments a method of getting rid of the gloom of the low-windowed, Early English triforium, which, although perfectly successful within the church, would, if it had been carried throughout, have been productive of a most injurious effect upon the appearance of the fabric within and without, as may be seen at present in the compartments in question."[45] This method was to remove entirely the triforium roof, and to convert the open arcade of the triforium towards the church into windows by filling the tracery with glass. The designer thus introduced a flood of light upon the choir altar, the shrines in the neighbourhood, and Bishop Barnet's tomb under the pier arch, which is beneath one of these windows. Fortunately the experiment was not repeated. After some time had elapsed, the changes above indicated were carried out; the low Early English triforium outer wall was removed, and the loftier Decorated wall and windows erected. In the extract above given it looks as if the removal of the triforium roof, putting a lead roof to the aisle below, and turning the triforium arches into windows, were confined to these two bays on the south. But the same thing was also done in the two corresponding bays on the north. But there, when the later raising of the triforium walls took place, this raised wall was continued over the two bays in question; and we do not now see there any remains of Early English work.

---

[45] Professor Willis's observations upon this subject are given in Stewart's "Architectural History," pp. 76-81.

THE PRIOR'S DOORWAY.

Photochrom Co. Ltd. Photo.

THE SOUTH TRANSEPT

In the east wall of the **South Transept** are broad, geometrical windows of two lights each. At the top of the southern face of this transept, deeply recessed, is an extraordinary Perpendicular window of seven lights. There seems no record of this being constructed. By the remains of corbels in the lower part of the wall we see that there was once a covered passage here, no doubt connecting the cloister with the chapter-house.

Beyond the transept are three Norman doors of exceptional interest. One, indeed, is in the west side of the transept, and must have been the original entrance here into the church. It is now quite blocked up with stone. It has only recently been discovered. There are remains of two Norman doors, the lower, with enriched mouldings and shaft, being considerably later in date than the round arch above it. This latter has the nail-head ornament. The northern end of the arch is concealed, as well as the eastern end of the adjoining door into the south aisle, by a mass of masonry built for a buttress.

THE MONKS' DOOR

The door into the south aisle is known as **The Monks' Door**, and is the regular entrance into the cathedral from the south. It opened from the eastern walk of the cloister. It is of later date than the wall in which it is placed. The ornamentation is very rich; one spiral column is especially noteworthy. There is a trefoiled arch, the cusps having circular terminations with the star ornament. In the spandrels are quaint, crouching monks, each holding a pastoral staff. Above are two curiously twisted dragons.

THE PRIOR'S DOOR

The Prior's Door is nearly at the west end of the north alley of the cloister. Like the monks' door, it is an insertion, being later than the wall. It is a very fine specimen of late Norman. The tympanum is filled with carving in high relief. In the centre is the Saviour, seated, enclosed within a *vesica piscis*, His right hand uplifted in blessing, His left hand resting on an open book; His bare feet rest upon the border of the oval enclosure. This oval is supported by two angels, the arms which hold the upper part being abnormally lengthened. On each side is a round shaft, enriched with a deeply cut series of ornaments running in a spiral; and at the head is a cushion capital with interlacing ornamentation. On each side of the shaft is a square pillar, the outer one having some curious figures of beasts and other objects enclosed in circular rings, while the foliage of the inner one is singularly like a premature specimen of Early English conventional decoration. The topmost stone of this inner jamb is enlarged into a corbel to support the lintel, and is carved with a large face. The expense of the restoration of this doorway was undertaken by the Bedfordshire Architectural Society.[46]

THE CLOISTER

One or two bays of the north alley of **The Cloister** have been lately restored by Canon Dickson as a vestry for the choir-boys. These are not, of course, now open to the air. Against the wall of the church can be seen the Norman arcading, showing there were cloisters from the first; while the remains of the windows towards the cloister enclosure, to be seen in the north and east alleys, tell us that they were rebuilt in the Perpendicular period, probably in the last quarter of the

[46] Bishop Goodwin's "Ely Gossip," 1892, p. 48.

fifteenth century. Some corbels remain in the wall of the cathedral. The roof of the cloister was therefore of wood; but there are remains of vaulting to the west of the prior's door, so perhaps the western alley had a stone roof. The first window to the west of the prior's door is original Norman; all the rest (except one) were changed into three light windows, apparently of the same date as those in the north aisle, but have lately been reconstructed in the Norman style. This applies only to the windows in the aisle; those in the triforium are of three lights, similar to those removed from the aisle; and those in the clerestory are the original Norman, just as on the north side.

THE NAVE, LOOKING WEST.
Photochrom Co. Ltd. Photo.

S. CATHARINE'S CHAPEL.

Photochrom Co. Ltd. Photo.

CHAPTER III.

THE CATHEDRAL: INTERIOR.

Entering the cathedral from the west, we have the full view of the entire building, the vista being not broken, but relieved, by the open screen. Before examining the nave itself, the visitor should inspect the lower part of the west tower, beneath which he is standing. The curious labyrinth worked in the pavement was there placed by Sir G. G. Scott, and is believed to have been designed by him, and not copied from any foreign example. The troubles that arose from the great weight of the tower have been already described. We can here see the methods taken to secure the stability of the structure.[47] Very massive Perpendicular arches have been built beneath the lofty Norman ones; and all the four great piers were surrounded with masonry at the same time. Both Bentham and Miller give the date 1405-1406 for the beginning of this work. This date is quite consistent with the character of the mouldings of the arches. There was at one time a plaster ceiling just above

---

[47] Quite recently further security has been attained by a system of iron bracing, not visible from beneath.

these lower arches.

Above the inner west door is a series of panels bearing coats of arms, so much resembling the fronts of galleries built for the accommodation of instrumental performers—which were known as "Minstrels' galleries"—as to suggest the idea that the large room over the porch was devoted to this purpose. The window above is an unfortunate insertion, dating only from 1800; and this, as well as the stained glass with which it is filled, could well be spared.

THE WESTERN TRANSEPT AND S. CATHARINE'S CHAPEL

The Western Transept and **S. Catharine's Chapel.**—The Transitional character of the late Norman work here is more marked than on the outside of the west front. It will be noticed that the great arches of the tower, though retaining all other characteristics of the period, are pointed. There are two rows of mouldings, and in the spandrels above are pointed ovals. Above the string-course are three stages: the lowest has three sets of lofty trefoiled lancets, supported by double detached shafts; above is a similar series, less lofty; at the top are three large glazed windows. The painted ceiling of the tower was Mr. le Strange's first experiment in painting at Ely. Some ancient decoration in the vault of the south aisle of the nave had been brought to light when he was on a visit at the Deanery, and this to some extent suggested the thought of painting the flat roof of the tower. The subject is the Creation. We see the right hand of the Lord; the Saviour holding a globe, surrounded by the heavenly bodies of the fourth day of the Creation; the Holy Dove; angels holding scrolls, with the Trisagion; and all these are in circular designs, united by branches of foliage. A very sad accident occurred during the early period of the restoration of the tower in 1845, when Mr. Basevi, the architect, met his death by falling from the upper floor of the scaffold which had been erected for the work. He was buried in the cathedral, and a brass has been laid over his grave. He was not in any way professionally connected with the work of the restoration.

The very late appearance of the highly enriched work in the south part of the western transept makes it probable that this part was completed in quite the latest years of the twelfth century. The zigzag mouldings to the two arches in the east are of extraordinary richness; one opens to the south aisle, and one to S. Catharine's chapel. The whole of this arm of the transept was at one time walled off, and the chapel itself was destroyed. This has been rebuilt, under the advice and authority of Professor Willis. The Woodford Trustees of the Theological College were at the expense of providing the alabaster altar; and the chapel is now used for the daily service of the members of that college, as well as for early celebrations of Holy Communion. Although now known as S. Catharine's chapel, it has never, strictly speaking, been so dedicated; and the present Dean has pointed out that the name was given under a misapprehension. The font in the transept was the gift of Canon Selwyn. Its style is in keeping with the adjacent architecture. The north portion of the western transept is entirely walled off. No documentary evidence has been discovered to decide if it had been actually built. The old tradition of the cathedral was that it had been finished by Bishop Eustace at the beginning of the thirteenth century.

THE NAVE, LOOKING EAST.

THE NAVE

The Nave.—Originally of thirteen bays, but since the fall of the central tower of twelve bays, the nave is a most complete and perfect specimen of late Norman work. The naves of Ely and Peterborough are conspicuously the best examples of the period in England. In most respects they are very similar, and it would be difficult to pronounce one superior to the other. In one point, indeed, the superiority is with the Ely nave. There is not in it the slightest mixture of any Transitional details. At Peterborough we can detect, towards the west, some unmistakable evidences of the approaching change in style.

It is believed that the nave was completed in the time of Bishop Riddell—that is, before 1173. This is probably somewhat earlier than the nave at Peterborough; but both were obviously being built at the same time for the greater part of the period of their erection. Both are manifestly superior to Norwich, where (to mention only one point) the excessive height of the triforium arches and the comparative low elevation of the nave arches—so that the two arcades are almost of the same dimensions—produce an unpleasing effect. But the work at Norwich was earlier, perhaps by thirty years, than either of the others. It is very difficult to obtain exact and authoritative measurements; but those usually given supply the following comparison:—Norwich, 14 bays; length of nave, 250 feet: Peterborough, 11 bays; length of nave, 228 feet: Ely, 12 bays; length of nave, 208 feet. From this it will be seen that before the tower fell the naves of Ely and Peterborough were almost exactly of the same length, while the former had two more bays than the latter.

The piers are of alternate design. In front of each an inner shaft runs up to the roof. The string-course above the main arcade has the billet moulding. All the attached shafts in all three stages have cushion capitals. Under each of the large triforium arches are two smaller ones. Though it has been said that there is no trace of any change of style throughout the entire nave, yet it has been noticed that there is a certain roughness about the execution of the arches towards the east which is not seen further west. The floors of the nave and its aisles are on one level; but till recently the floors of the aisles were a few inches lower, and this is believed to have been the original arrangement. The clerestory range has three arches, the central being the highest.

THE CEILING

The western half of the **ceiling** was painted by Mr. Styleman le Strange, of Hunstanton Hall, in Norfolk, between 1858 and 1861. He died in 1862. The eastern half was then undertaken by Mr. Gambler Parry, of Highnam Court, near Gloucester; and the main design of Mr. le Strange was carried to a most successful issue. The original idea had been that a Jesse tree should commence at the seventh bay, and the arrangement of the subjects towards the west was meant to lead up to this. But Mr. le Strange himself, as the work proceeded, realised that a grander effect would be produced by introducing larger scriptural subjects towards the east; and Mr. Gambier Parry accordingly acted upon what was known to be the intention of the original designer. It has been many times said that the whole design was suggested by the painted ceiling at Hildesheim, and some words of Sir G. G. Scott have been quoted as proof of this; but Dean Goodwin says that the scheme was not taken in any way from the foreign example, and that Mr. le Strange had not seen the Hildesheim ceiling when his design was formed.[48] It is worth noting that some of the faces of the prophets are portraits; that of Isaiah, for instance, is a portrait of Dean Peacock. The general tone of the colouring is intentionally subdued, and the effect of this is said to be to increase the apparent height of the nave.

PANELS IN THE NAVE CEILING.

Photochrom Co. Ltd. Photo.

The twelve subjects along the central portion of the ceiling, commencing at the west, are these: (1) The Creation, (2) The Fall, (3) The Sacrifice of Noah, (4) The Sacrifice of Isaac, (5) Jacob's Dream, (6) The Marriage of Ruth, (7) Jesse, (8) David, (9) The Annunciation, (10) The Nativity, (11) The Adoration of the Shepherds and of the Magi, (12) The Lord in Glory.[49]

[48] "Ely Gossip," p. 39.

[49] When Murray's "Eastern Cathedrals" was published, Mr. Gambier Parry's work had not been begun; and by comparing the above list with the list there given as the proposed series of sacred subjects for the last six bays of the ceiling, it will be seen that the last three subjects are not the same as at first intended.

On the inner slope on each side of the central line for the ten western bays are figures of patriarchs and prophets, each with a scroll bearing some of his own words, all having prophetic reference to the Messiah. On the outer slope on each side are heads in circular medallions, three in each bay. "The heads forming the border represent the human ancestors of our Lord, according to the genealogy in S. Luke's Gospel; they commence at the eastern end and terminate at the western, thus linking together the Glorified Manhood, as exhibited in the last of the pictorial representations, with the Creation of Man in the first."[50]

The sloping sides of the ceiling follow the course of the great beams supporting the roof. Till it was resolved to construct this ceiling the beams were exposed, and the whole was open to the leads. Canon Stewart speaks of it as a "remarkable example of a trussed rafter roof of seven cants," and says that such a roof was sometimes called a compass roof. He thinks it might have taken the place of an original roof of the thirteenth century.

THE NORTH AISLE OF THE NAVE.

Photochrom Co. Ltd. Photo.

THE NAVE AISLES

The Nave Aisles.—These retain their groined roofs. Some remains of coloured decoration may be seen in various places, especially in the south aisle; and the appearance of more elaborate colouring at one place seems to indicate that there was a side altar beneath. The rood-screen in the nave was by the pier in which is

[50] From the key to the ceiling by Dean Stubbs, in "Handbook," 20th ed., pp. 60, 61.

a small canopied niche. In the north aisle, beneath the windows, is an arcade of round-headed lancets, four in each bay. Above the arcade was originally a string of chevron moulding running along the whole length of the aisle; but this has been hacked off, except beneath the most eastern window. In the south aisle there are five such lancets in each bay west of the prior's door, and four in each bay beyond. The windows east of this door are higher in the wall than the others, because of the cloister, and the wall arcade is correspondingly more lofty. The chevron moulding remains in this aisle for seven bays, after which (until the last bay but one) the marks of it are clearly to be seen. One of the windows in the south aisle is original; all the rest, except one, have been recently made like it. In the north aisle all the windows are of the Perpendicular period, and have three lights under ogee arches. All are filled with stained glass.

THE SOUTH AISLE OF THE NAVE.

Photochrom Co. Ltd. Photo.

In the south aisle is placed an ancient memorial stone of the greatest interest. It consists of the square base and part of the shaft of a cross. It was brought here from Haddenham, where it had been used as a horse-block, by Mr. Bentham. On the base is this inscription:

LVCEM TVAM OVINO
DA DEVS ET REQVIE(M)
AMEN.

Ovin has been named in the account of the foundress as being her chief agent, to whom was entrusted the civil government of her territory. There is every reason to believe that this cross was erected either by him or to his memory; and if so it must be twelve centuries old.

Just west of the monks' door is the entrance to the recently constructed vestry for the choir-boys. This is thought to have been originally the entrance to the cloister library or bookcase.

THE OCTAGON

The Octagon.—Few visitors will perhaps be disposed to examine any of the objects of interest in the cathedral before an inspection of the beauties of this magnificent erection, the first sight of which, from one of the smaller arches towards the aisles, is a thing never to be forgotten. There is not one of the many able artists and architects who have written about the octagon that has not spoken of it as being without rival in the whole world; and the admiration that was expressed fifty and more years ago would have been far greater, and the enthusiasm more profound, had the writers seen it in its present state of perfect restoration. No description can do adequate justice to the grandeur of the conception or to the brilliancy of the execution of this renowned work.

The four great arches rise to the full height of the roof; that to the east, indeed, is higher than the vaulted roof of the choir and presbytery, the intervening space being occupied with tracery of wood-work on painted boards, the Saviour on the Cross being painted in the middle. The wooden vaulting of the octagon springs from capitals on the same level as those of the great arches. The four small arches to the aisles are of course no higher than the roofs of the aisles: above these, on each side, are three figures of apostles, under canopies with crockets. The figures are seated, and each holds an emblem, by which it can be seen for whom the figure is intended. It may be noticed (in the central figure on the south-west side) that S. Paul, not S. Matthias, is put in the place of Iscariot. The hood-moulds of the arches are terminated by heads, of which six are portraits. King Edward III. and Queen Philippa are at the north-east, Bishop Hotham and Prior Crauden at the southeast, Walsingham and his master mason (so it is believed) at the north-west; those to the south-west are mere grotesques. Above the seated figures on each side is a window of four broad lights, filled with stained glass. The eight chief vaulting shafts rise from the ground as slight triple shafts; they support, a little above the spring of the side arches, large corbels, which form bases for exquisitely designed niches, and through these spring more shafts reaching to the vault. On each of the corbels is a boldly carved scene from the career of S. Etheldreda; they commence at the north-west arch. The subjects (two to each arch) are as follows:

NORTH-WEST ARCH.—S. Etheldreda's second marriage. Her taking the veil at Coldingham.

NORTH-EAST ARCH.—Her staff taking root. Her preservation in the flood at S. Abb's Head.

SOUTH-EAST ARCH.—Her installation as Abbess of Ely, Her

death and burial (two scenes).

SOUTH-WEST ARCH.—One of her miracles. Her translation.

All these incidents have been sufficiently explained in the chapter on the history of the building, with the exception of the seventh. The authority for this is the "Liber Eliensis." A man named Brytstan,[51] being ill, had vowed that if he were restored to health he would become a monk. Upon his taking steps to carry out this intention he was charged with seeking refuge in a monastery simply to escape the consequences of robberies of which he had been guilty in his business. After trial at Huntingdon he was condemned and put in chains in prison in London. After continuous prayers for the intercession of S. Etheldreda and S. Benedict, these two saints appeared to him, and the latter drew the links of the chain apart and set the prisoner free. The miracle came to the knowledge of Matilda, Henry I.'s queen, and investigations followed, which resulted in the release of Brytstan, and he was conducted to Ely with manifestations of joy. Some have thought that the ribands still to be bought at the stalls at the annual fair, and known as "S. Audrey's laces," are a reminiscence of this legend, and that they represent the chains from which Brytstan was delivered. But the more probable explanation is that they refer to the disease that afflicted S. Etheldreda, a swelling in the neck, which she held to be a fit punishment for the vanity of her youthful days, when she was fond of wearing necklaces and jewels. "Saint Audrey's laces" became corrupted into "Tawdry laces"; and so the adjective has been applied to all cheap and showy pieces of female ornament.

Special attention may be given to some points in the sculpture of these corbels, every one of which is worthy of careful study. In (1) notice the figure of Ovin, previously named as the steward, bearing an official staff, or perhaps a sword. In (2) the surrender of royal dignity is signified by the crown placed on the altar. In (3) the leaf-bearing staff has an abundance of conventional foliage. In (5) Wilfrid bears a simple pastoral staff, and not an archbishop's cross, as in previous scenes—a point to which Dean Stubbs calls attention as indicating the historical accuracy of the designer, because in former scenes the archbishop is represented in his own diocese, while here he is a simple bishop in banishment. In (6) there is a dignified figure—probably S. Sexburga—standing behind the priest who is ministering to the dying abbess. In (7) the kneeling figure is S. Benedict handling the fetters.

---

[51] Admirable and exhaustive descriptions of these pieces of sculpture, with sketches of six of them, are given in Dean Stubbs' "Historical Memorials of Ely Cathedral," pp. 71-84. The account in the text of the miracle on the seventh corbel is condensed from this description.

THE SOUTH TRANSEPT.

Photochrom Co. Ltd. Photo.

Until the plain colour-wash with which the vault had been covered was removed in 1850 there was no knowledge of what had been the character of the original decoration. Traces of colouring were then discovered, and in some places geometrical designs, but there was no evidence of anything very elaborate. The whole

of the present decoration forms accordingly an entirely new design; it is by Mr. Gambier Parry, who himself painted the principal figures. The central boss of the lantern is carved in oak, and is original; only its painting is new. All the remaining figures are wholly new. Groups of seraphim, bands of heavenly minstrels bearing all kinds of ancient musical instruments, monograms, and sacred emblems, all combine to give a rich variety.

THE NORTH TRANSEPT.

Photochrom Co. Ltd. Photo.

THE TRANSEPTS

The Transepts.—The architectural student will find the transepts of the greatest interest; as in them is to be seen the earliest work in the cathedral. They are similar in general character to those at Winchester, which were built by Abbot Simeon's brother. The transepts at Winchester were ready for consecration in 1093, and this was seven years before Simeon came to Ely. The triforium is probably only in part Simeon's work; and the clerestory was almost certainly added by his successor. Both transepts have aisles, but in the south transept the western aisle is walled off. Along the western wall in the north transept is a stone bench. The square capitals of the piers here have indentations at the corners, and this is an early example of such indentation. Some slight ornamentation may be noticed in the cushions of the capitals, especially in the south transept, where there are traces of ancient colouring. The three chapels to the east of the north transept are divided by walls, and two have wooden screens. One of these has been restored by Professor Stanton for use as a chapel for early celebrations and for private devotion. Some early paintings on the vaulted roof, representing the martyrdom of S. Edmund, are sufficient to justify this being called S. Edmund's chapel. It is probable that this was the Chantry on the Green (so called from the place of residence of the four chaplains) founded by Bishop Northwold. The screen in front of this chapel is exceedingly light and graceful; it dates from about 1350. At one time it is said to have been in the south transept, and afterwards where it now stands; it was removed in 1865, but is now replaced. In the south transept the whole of the eastern aisle is walled off for the library. In the plan in Bentham's History, 1770, only the single bay to the south is marked as the library. The walls of partition between the chapels were taken down in 1814. The western aisle has always been separated by a low wall of Norman date, possibly a little later than the adjacent piers; this wall has an intersecting arcade of round arches, with a string of chevrons above. This aisle is used as a vestry. Within is the ancient Norman vaulting; and there are some good original windows, which cannot be seen from without except from the Deanery gardens. From the devices on the late Perpendicular door it is clear that it belonged to some church erected by Bishop Alcock; it was only brought here from Landbeach about fifty years ago.

The triforium and clerestory ranges are almost identical with those in the nave. In the south transept the western windows of the triforium have been altered into three-light Perpendicular windows. The roofs of both transepts have been raised, but it is not known at what time. At the north end are two large windows of good Perpendicular character; at the south is a single window of seven lights, of very singular design. At the ends of the transepts are two original galleries, level with the triforium, supported on round-headed arches. On the north are five arches, not of equal height, the two most lofty of which reach nearly to the triforium level. On the south are six much lower arches, and above them is a blank arcade of intersecting arches. In the floor of the south transept are laid some very remarkable ancient tiles.

THE CHOIR SCREEN.

Photochrom Co. Ltd. Photo.

THE CHOIR AND PRESBYTERY

The Choir and **Presbytery**—A beautiful screen of oak, with brass gates, designed by Scott, divides the choir from the octagon. It is of early geometric character; and if there had been an original screen of this design it would have been intermediate in date between the presbytery and the choir. The tracery is very graceful. A rich cresting runs along the top, cut through by the gable over the gates, which bears a terminal cross. On both sides the small niches have statuettes.

ELEVATION OF THE BAYS OF THE PRESBYTERY.

(for exterior see p. 40.)

The choir, of three bays, is the work of Bishop Hotham. The last six bays are the work of Bishop Northwold, and form the presbytery. In the present arrangement seven of these nine bays form the ritual choir, and two form the retro-choir. The difference in date between the presbytery and choir may be roughly taken as very nearly a hundred years. The former had been begun in 1240; the latter was nearly finished in 1340. In the juxtaposition of these two magnificent specimens of the Early English and Decorated periods of architecture there is an opportunity of comparison which on such a scale occurs nowhere else. It is to be remembered that in neither case is the treatment of the upper part quite in accordance with the usual practice of the period. When the presbytery was being built there were still standing east of the central tower the four original bays of the Norman choir. These, it may be assumed, were very similar in character to those in the nave. There would, beyond question, have been in each bay large triforium arches, each with a couple of subordinate arches; and a single window in the clerestory with a blank arch on each side. Bishop Northwold's work was purposely made to correspond with these bays as far as Early English work could do so; and when after the fall of the tower it became necessary to rebuild the choir, Bishop Hotham in like manner made his Decorated work correspond with the Early English presbytery. The choir is, as would be expected, richer in detail as well as more elaborate in design; and it would be difficult to find in England anything to surpass the tracery of the clerestory windows and triforium arches, the beautiful cusped inner arches of the clerestory range, the open parapets at the base of the two stages, or the long corbels, covered with foliage, that support the vaulting shafts. In the choir the clerestory windows have four lights each; in the presbytery are triplets. The old colouring has been renewed throughout. On the north side of the choir the three bays are precisely alike; but on the south there is a variation in the tracery of the western triforium arch. There are also shields of arms (of the See of Ely and of Bishop Hotham) in the spandrels of the triforium and arch below; and the shaft between this arch and the next is enlarged at the top into a base for a statue (probably of S. Etheldreda); while level with the string above is a very fine large canopy (called by the work-men "the table"), which is like nothing else in the cathedral. The clerestory windows also on the south have different tracery.

THE CHOIR, LOOKING WEST.

Photochrom Co. Ltd. Photo.

The difference between the two styles of architecture is well marked in the groining of the roof, the Decorated portion being much more elaborate. Some of the bosses are very remarkable: one has S. Etheldreda with pastoral staff; one has the coronation of the Virgin Mary; one has the foundress bearing the model of a church, in which (as Dean Stubbs has pointed out) both arms of the western transept are represented, so that it is a fair inference that at the time this roof was constructed the whole of the western transept was standing.

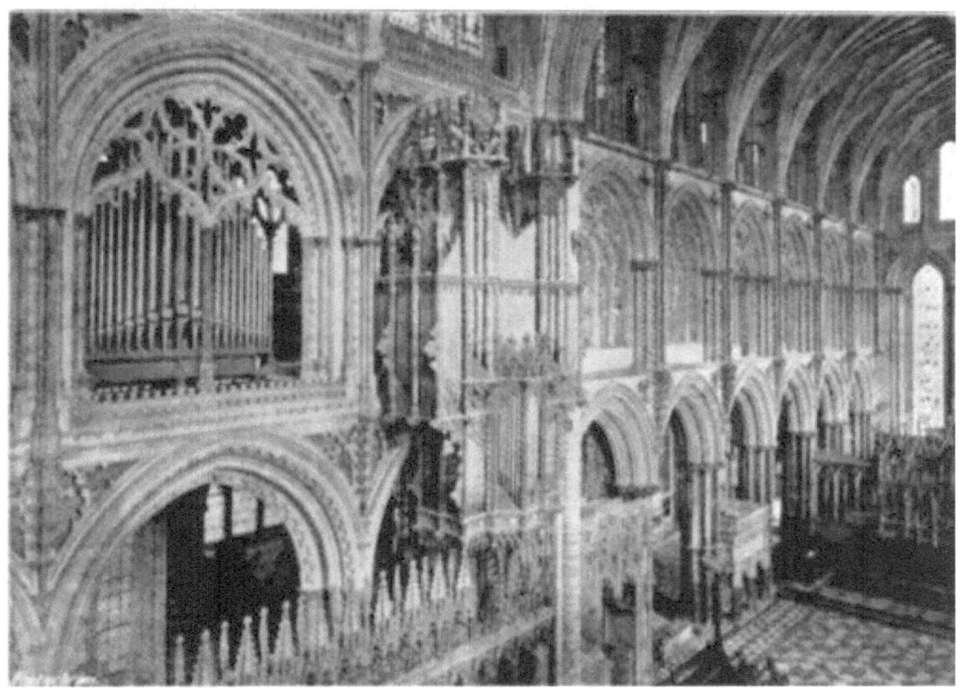

THE TRIFORIUM OF THE CHOIR AND PRESBYTERY.

Photochrom Co. Ltd. Photo.

Between the choir and presbytery there rise the massive Norman piers built as the entrance to the apse; and these are the only remains of the Norman church east of the octagon. Since the careful examination of the foundations here, made by Professor Willis in 1850, it is not thought certain that the apse was actually built. The foundations of the apse were very manifest, and the design did not include a passage round it; but there was also clear evidence that the apsidal foundation was altered into a straight wall of the same thickness, and the probability is that before the apse was built "it was resolved to convert it into a square-ended presbytery, such as we now see at Oxford Cathedral and St. Cross."[52]

---

[52] Canon Stewart, in *The Builder*, April 2nd, 1892.

THE CHOIR STALLS: NORTH SIDE.

Photochrom Co. Ltd. Photo.

The two most western triforium arches in the presbytery are glazed, the roof of the triforium itself being wholly removed. The object of this alteration has been fully explained in the account of the exterior of the cathedral. On the ground beneath were the shrines; and under one of the arches was erected, not long afterwards, the monument of Bishop Barnet, in whose time and at whose expense the alteration was made.

The arrangement of the lancets at the east end is even more effective within than without. The east end of Ely, says Professor Freeman, "is the grandest example of the grouping of lancets.... Ely is also undoubtedly the head of all east ends and eastern limbs of that class in which the main body of the church is of the same height throughout, and in which the aisles are brought out to the full length of the building."[53]

THE REREDOS.

Photochrom Co. Ltd. Photo.

It will hardly be believed that the magnificent stalls which were formerly ranged in the octagon, and at a later period in the presbytery, were once painted all over with a mahogany colour. They are the finest Decorated stalls in England, the beautiful ones at Winchester being of late thirteenth-century date. The carved panels in the upper parts are new, and are the gifts of individual donors. They were executed in Belgium. It is not known how these spaces were originally filled; Mr. le Strange thought possibly with heraldic devices. The designs on the south

[53] Introduction to Farren's "Cathedral Cities of Ely and Norwich."

are from the New Testament, those on the north from the Old Testament The seats in the lower range are also modern, as are the various statuettes at the Stall ends, which represent the builders of the most important parts of the fabric. On the misereres of the ancient stalls are some wonderful grotesque carvings. The brass eagle lectern has been copied, as to its main features, from an ancient example at Isleham. The organ is in the triforium, on the north, and part of the case projects over the easternmost arch of the choir.

The reredos is the first example in modern cathedral work of the elaborate style of decoration for the most holy part of the sanctuary, which is now not uncommon. It was the gift of Mr. John Dunn Gardner, of Chatteris, and was designed by Scott. It forms the central portion of a screen of stone which extends for the whole width of the presbytery. The lower part of the whole is of deeply cut diaper-work; the upper part has an open arcade of six arches, each with a mullion and tracery in the early Decorated style. The reredos itself is of alabaster, and consists of five main arches under canopies, and with tracery, and is ornamented with a rich abundance of mosaic work, panels, medallions, statuettes, twisted columns, and various kinds of carving. Five scenes from the last days of our Lord's life on earth are carved in relief under canopies beneath the chief arches. A full description, giving all the details of the sculpture, and the materials of the mosaic, and the different persons and emblematic graces represented by the busts and figures, would require more space than we can give. The altar cross, of silver gilt, is in memory of Bishop Woodford.

THE LADY-CHAPEL

The Lady-chapel.—Notwithstanding the cruel mutilation of the sculpture all round this chapel, it can be seen that for perfection of exquisite work there is no building of the size in this country worthy for one moment to be compared with this in its unmutilated state. Its single defect strikes the beholder at once: the span of the roof is too broad and the vaulting too depressed for the size of the chapel. The windows, of which those on the north have been restored, have already been described. The end windows, which are of great size, are of later date; that to the east has a look of Transition work about it. The building was finished in 1349, and the east window was inserted by Bishop Barnet, *circa* 1373. For a possible explanation of the insertion of this window, only a quarter of a century after the completion of the chapel, see *ante*, p. 52. It is not thought probable that the original designers left anything incomplete. The great beauty of the interior consists in the series of tabernacle work and canopies that runs round all the four sides below and between the windows. The heads of the canopies project. In the tracery beneath, at the head of the mullion, was a statue. The delicate carving of the cusps and other tracery is varied throughout. On the spandrels were incidents connected with the history of the Virgin Mary (mainly legendary) and of Julian the Apostate; and though in no single instance is a perfect uninjured specimen left, yet enough remains, in all but a few cases, for the original subjects to be identified.[54] All was

[54] For a full account and list of all the subjects as far as is known, see Dean Stubbs' catalogue of them, abridged from Dr. Montagu James' work on the iconography of the lady-chapel, given in the "Handbook," 20th ed., pp. 127-132.

once enriched with colour, and many traces remain; and in various parts of the windows there are fragments of stained glass. Most of the monumental tablets which once disfigured the arcade below the windows have been happily removed into the vestibule. The arches and canopies at the east end are arranged differently from those on the sides. In the roof, which reminds us of the contemporary roof in the choir, are some carved bosses, not large, but singularly good. Among the subjects can be recognised a Crucifixion, with half-figures beside the cross; Adam and Eve; the Virgin Mary and Elizabeth, holding between them a book inscribed "Magnificat"; the Annunciation, with "Ave Maria Gracia plena"; the Ascension, indicated by the skirt and feet of the Saviour and five heads of apostles; the coronation of the Virgin; and the Virgin in an aureole.

THE LADY-CHAPEL.

Photochrom Co. Ltd. Photo.

The arrangements for worship present an appearance very unlike those of sixty years ago. A writer in 1876, writing of his early recollections, says: "When I first knew Ely the state of the lady-chapel—then, as now, used as a parish church—was so miserable from decay, violence, and neglect, that it was simply painful to enter it." ... Now, "well-designed benches have replaced the mean deal square pews, the whitewash and yellow-wash which thickly clogged the carving has been removed, the windows have been repaired and made water-tight, and the altar and its adjuncts made to assume an air of reverent dignity."

DOORWAY OF THE LADY-CHAPEL.

Rev. T. Perkins Photo.

We do not remember to have anywhere seen an explanation of the fact that this chapel is now used as the parish church of Holy Trinity parish; whereas the old church, the destruction of which occasioned the appropriation of the lady-chapel to parochial use, was dedicated to S. Cross.

MONUMENTS AND STAINED GLASS

Monuments And Stained Glass—It is convenient to treat the monuments as a separate subject, so as not to break the continuity of the architectural description. We will commence at the west, proceeding along the north aisle, and so round the cathedral, pointing out those that have anything of special interest.

Against the blocked doorway which gave access to the church of S. Cross is placed an altar-tomb to the late Bishop Woodford (see below, p. 129). The figure of the bishop is vested in cope and mitre, and has a pastoral staff. The Crucifixion is on the wall at the back. There are several shields of arms relating to the bishop's career or to the cathedral history: among these are those of the Merchant Taylors' Company, at whose school he was educated; Pembroke College, Cambridge, of which he was a member; and of other colleges at Cambridge founded by bishops of Ely. Three tablets in this north aisle, near the transept, record donations towards the re-paving of the nave and aisles in 1676, 1869, and 1873.

There is no monumental memorial in the nave. But the large slab of marble in the centre, just in front of the position of the old rood-loft, which has been already referred to as traditionally marking the grave of Alan de Walsingham, should be noticed.

Under the four arches of the presbytery on the north, between the stalls and the altar, are monuments of great importance. First we see that of Bishop Redman (d. 1505), a very fine specimen of enriched Perpendicular work. The mitred figure of the bishop is on an altar-tomb beneath a richly groined roof, and a space is left at the feet, where a priest might stand to pray for the soul of the deceased prelate.[55] There are grand canopies on the sides, with crockets and coloured shields bearing emblems of the Crucifixion, the arms of the See of Ely and of S. Asaph, where Bishop Redman was at first; but the arms of the See of Exeter, from which diocese he came to Ely, as now used, are not to be seen. Above the roof is fine open screen-work, and against the adjoining piers, east and west, are large canopied niches.

Next to this is the effigy of Bishop Kilkenny (d. 1256), a fine example of Early English. The figure has cope, mitre, and staff. The bishop's heart only was buried here.

In the next arch is a large Decorated structure of two stories, believed by Scott to have been built by Walsingham as the base for the shrine of S. Etheldreda. It was formerly known as Bishop Hotham's shrine, and his effigy was placed beneath it. The lower story is open.

In the arch north of the altar is the tomb of the builder of the presbytery, Bishop Northwold (d. 1254). He is represented in full vestments. At the east of the tomb is a curious carving, apparently meant for the martyrdom of S. Edmund. A king naked above the middle, except for his kingly crown, is tied to a tree and pierced by arrows; archers with drawn bows are behind; at one end the king has his head,

[55] In the inventory of plate, etc., "belonging to the late priory at Ely," made 31 Hen. VIII., printed in Bentham's "History" from the MS. in Corpus Christi College, Cambridge, the only altars mentioned are the high altar, those in the lady-chapel, in the chapels of Bishops Alcock and West, and in "Byslope Redmannes Chaple."

still crowned, in his hands, with a figure bearing a sword over him; at the other side is either the wolf of the legend or an evil spirit in animal shape.

THE NORTH CHOIR AISLE.

In the aisle itself are several memorials, mostly of the eighteenth century, that call for no special mention. The latest is the brass to Mr. Basevi, 1845.

THE CHAPEL OF BISHOP ALCOCK

At the east end of the aisle is the **Chapel Of Bishop Alcock** (d. 1500). The date, 1488, is fixed precisely by the inscribed stone now placed in the wall above a small stone altar. The stone in the wall has five crosses, as though intended for a chantry altar, but the slab of the altar beneath has no crosses. The inscription is, "Iohanes Alkoc epus Eliesis hanc fabricam fieri fecit M cccc iiij(xx) viij." The sides of the chapel are covered with niches, canopies, crockets, panels, and devices. The roof has fan tracery with a massive pendant. A singular little chantry is at the north, access to which is through a door at the foot of the bishop's tomb. In a small window here is a little contemporary stained glass. The bishop's rebus—a cock on a globe—repeatedly occurs in the stone-work. The ornamentation strikes the spectator as being excessive and too profuse. No figures have been replaced in the niches.

In the retro-choir a mosaic slab over the remains of Bishop Allen (d. 1845) has a curious history. A son of the bishop was passing through Paris soon after Napoleon's tomb was finished, and the surplus materials were offered for sale by auction. Some of these were purchased by Mr. Allen and utilised for the slab over the bishop's grave. The large monument to Canon Mill (d. 1853) has an effigy in copper on a support of marble and alabaster; students of India and Cambridge are by the feet.

THE EARLY ENGLISH PRESBYTERY AND THE SUPPOSED SHRINE OF S. ETHELDREDA.

The tomb of Cardinal Luxemburg (d. 1443) is beneath the most eastern arch on the south, just north of Bishop West's chapel. When the monument was concealed behind some wood-work great dispute arose as to the headdress of the effigy. Bentham has an engraving with a cardinal's hat on the archbishop's head. Cole records that it was a mitre. When the wood-work was removed it was found that the figure was headless, as it still remains.

THE CHAPEL OF BISHOP WEST

Corresponding to the chapel of Bishop Alcock on the north is that of **Bishop West** (d. 1533) in the south aisle. This is a most valuable example of the Renaissance style. The niches and canopies with which the walls are covered are much smaller than those in the other chapel, and consequently more numerous; but by reason of the great delicacy of the tracery and the wonderful variety of the designs there is no impression that the decoration is overdone. No perfect specimen is left of the statues or of the heads which were introduced in the tabernacle work; and in its complete state this exquisite work can have existed for not more, than twelve or thirteen years, as the Order in Council for removing images was made in 1548. The roof is curious, as being an adaptation in the Renaissance of the late Gothic fan tracery Some colouring remains. The wrought-iron gates, with motto in Latin several times repeated, and the curious little pendants from the roof, consisting of angels bearing shields of arms, should be noticed. Bishops Greene (d. 1738), Keene (d. 1781), Sparke (d. 1836), and Woodford (d. 1885) are all buried in this chapel. On the south side, within a shrine-like receptacle, have been placed the relics of seven early benefactors of the church. Originally buried in the Saxon church, they have been several limes removed. They were placed here in 1771. The names are carved in seven shallow niches. One was an archbishop, five were bishops, and the seventh was Alderman Brithnoth. The dates range from 991 to 1067.

The very interesting early Norman monumental slab, with carving in relief, preserved in the aisle, does not strictly belong to the cathedral, having been found at S. Mary's Church. Above a round-headed canopy are some Norman buildings; in the chamfer of the canopy is an invocation of the Archangel Michael, a figure of whom below has wings and nimbus, and in the robe a portion of a naked figure with pastoral staff beside it.

Proceeding westward, the monuments under the windows are those of Canon Selwyn (d. 1875), Bishop Gunning (d. 1684), wearing a mitre, with long hair and short beard, and Bishop Heton (d. 1609), in a cope and having an ample beard. Under the arches of the presbytery, after the huge tablet to Bishop Moore (d. 1714), are four monuments. The first is all that is left of the tomb of Bishop Hotham (d. 1337). The next has figures of John Tiptoft, Earl of Worcester, K.G., and his two wives. The earl was beheaded in 1470, and is not interred here. One of the wives was Cecily Neville, sister of Richard, Earl of Warwick, the King-maker.

Of the tomb of Bishop Barnet (d. 1373) the base only remains. It resembles in general character the monument of Bishop Northwold.

Under the last arch of the presbytery is the fine monument of Bishop Louth (d.

1298). It is a very beautiful early Decorated composition.

BISHOP ALCOCK'S CHAPEL.

Two brasses remain in the floor of the south aisle, both of great interest. The famous brass of Bishop Goodrich (d. 1554) represents him in full vestments (wearing a chasuble, not a cope), with mitre and pastoral staff (see below, p. 124). This is specially noteworthy as he was an enthusiastic supporter of the Reformation changes and is believed to have encouraged, if he did not order the wholesale destruction of statues and other ornamentation of the cathedral. He was Lord Chancellor for three years, and the Great Seal is figured on the brass. Dean Tyndall (d. 1614) is represented in a very different style. He is figured in academical dress, wearing a ruff and a skull-cap, and with a long beard. On one of the shields of arms may be seen the arms of the Deanery impaling Tyndall.

BISHOP WEST'S CHAPEL.

Photochrom Co. Ltd. Photo.

Very many other tablets and inscriptions remain; but we have no space for a more extended treatment of the subject. In the south transept is a tablet to Dean Merivale (d. 1894), with a likeness in slight relief; and mention of this gives opportunity for saying that the very greatest care seems to have been taken to secure good likenesses in the most recent monuments, those of three, as to which the writer can speak from personal knowledge—Bishop Woodford, Dean Merivale, and Canon Selwyn—being of conspicuous merit.

It would require a book to itself to treat exhaustively of the stained glass in the windows. In nearly all cases, certainly in those which can be examined without the aid of a glass, the names of the donors, or of the persons to whose memory the windows were inserted, are plainly set forth either in the windows or on brass tablets adjoining. It should be stated that the greatest encouragement to this form of decoration was given by Canon E. B. Sparke, who secured, partly by his influence and persuasion, and largely by his own munificence, the insertion of so many windows. It is true that in the first instance not a few were prepared in too great a hurry, and some of those first placed in the restored cathedral (as those in the octagon) have been at a later time condemned as being deficient in harmony of colouring and in artistic design; but there is little fault to be found with the most recent additions. Among so many it is inevitable that very different degrees of merit will be exhibited. It has been said that the entire series is an exemplification of the Horatian maxim, "Sunt bona, sunt quædam mediocria, sunt mala plura"; and, except that we should be disposed to exchange the position of the words "quædam" and "plura" (if the metre allowed it), with this sentiment we agree.

THE CHOIR LOOKING EAST.

THE CHAPTER SEAL.

From Bentham.

CHAPTER IV.

HISTORY OF THE MONASTERY.

All that need be said of the original establishment at Ely has already been told in the account of the foundress. There is no doubt that in the monastery there were religious persons of both sexes. Dean Stubbs says "the mixed community was the fashion of the time"[56] and he gives Coldingham, Kildare, and three in Normandy—Chelles, Autun Brie, and Fontevrault—as examples of similar foundations. In this instance the abbess was the head of all; and this accounts for Bede's calling the house a nunnery. What name was given to the superior of the men's part does not appear.

Of all the abbesses who ruled over this "twin monastery" we know only the names of the first four; and all these were in due time canonised. These were S. Etheldreda (673-679), S. Sexburga (679-699), S. Ermenilda (699-?), and S. Werburga (dates unknown). If we allow ten years for the duration of the rule of the last two, we still have the names of the abbesses for only thirty-six years out of the one hundred and ninety-seven years that the institution lasted. It is said to have been in a very flourishing condition when the Danes came to destroy it; and there is no hint anywhere that there was not a continuous succession of abbesses during the whole period.

S. Sexburga, the elder sister of the foundress, succeeded her as abbess. She was the widowed queen of Ercombert, King of Kent, and had herself founded the monastery of Sheppey, at the place now known as Minster, and set over it her daughter

[56] "Memorials of Ely," p. 18. Gloucester is another example.

Ermenilda, another widowed queen. S. Sexburga joined the house at Ely, and had resided there some time before her sister's death. The body of S. Etheldreda was in her time removed into the church, under the superintendence of Archbishop Wilfrid. Bede gives a full account of the translation. The monks who had the charge of providing a stone coffin suitable for the reception of the remains of the foundress are said to have "found" one of marble among the ruins of Grantchester, the name of the old town of Cambridge. When disinterred, the body was reported free from all corruption. The account would not be complete without the customary miracles—marvellous cures effected by touching the clothes and coffin, and by the healing efficacy of a spring that flowed from the place of the first interment. This translation took place on October 17th, 695. This is the day assigned to the commemoration of S. Etheldreda. The importance of this festival is sometimes held to account for the fact that the Feast of S. Luke, on October 18th, is not preceded by a fast. But as no fast is assigned to the vigils of the Conversion of S. Paul, S. Mark, or Saints Philip and James, it is questionable if this opinion is sound. Upon the death of S. Sexburga, in 699, her body was laid in the church next to that of her sister.

The next abbess was her daughter, S. Ermenilda. Her husband had been Wulphere, King of Mercia, who died in 675. She had been professed at Ely, and left to become the head of her mother's foundation at Sheppey. The date of her death is not known. She was succeeded, both at Sheppey and at Ely, by her daughter, S. Werburga. How long she ruled at Ely is not recorded. She was buried by her own desire at Hanbury, in Staffordshire. When the Danes reached Derbyshire in their incursions, this was deemed no longer a safe place, and her body was removed to Chester, where the cathedral was afterwards placed under the joint invocation of S. Werburga and S. Oswald.[57] The reason why it is suggested above that ten years may be taken as the limit of time to be assigned to the rules of S. Ermenilda and S. Werburga is that the author of her Life[58] says that her body was taken up "9 years after her decease, to translate it to a more eminent part" of Hanbury Church, by order of Ceolred, King of Mercia. As this king died at latest in 1027, it would follow that S. Werburga must have died not later than 708.

Probably in the Isle of Ely more special respect was paid to the festivals of these four sainted abbesses than elsewhere. But we find no churches dedicated to any of the four in the isle except those previously named as dedicated to S. Etheldreda, the cathedral, Histon, and a chapel at Swaffham Prior. Minster Church, in Kent, is dedicated to Saints Mary and Sexburga. In a tenth-century will of the widowed queen of Edmund I. we read: "I give to S. Peter's, and to S. Ætheldryth, and to S. Wihtburh, and to S. Sexburh, and to S. Eormenhild at Ely where my lord's body rests, the three lands which we both promised to God and His saint."[59] There were no doubt side-altars erected in honour of one or more of the four. At Wisbech, for instance, there was a "light" of S. Etheldreda, to which we find per-

---

[57] "The Cathedral Church of Chester," in Bell's "Cathedral Series," p. 3.

[58] In MS., Corpus Christi College, Cambridge. Referred to by Bentham, p. 63.

[59] Quoted in "Fenland Notes and Queries," i., p. 163. The writer has found a will in the Probate Registry at Peterborough in which the testator, John Mobbe, of March, dates his will on the day of S. Ermenilda (February 13th), 1457.

sons bequeathing small sums.

Of the monastery of S. Etheldreda and that of Bishop Ethelwold, Professor Freeman writes that there is "no continuity between the two."[60] By this we must probably understand that he considered the original monastery absolutely at an end after its destruction by the Danes; and that the monastery founded in its place a century later was something quite new, that had no claim to be regarded as the continuation of the former one. But the history of the place during the interval was not an absolute blank.

The Danish destruction took place in 870. The reconstruction by King Edgar and Bishop Ethelwold took place in 970. In the monastery so founded, or, as most would prefer to say, resuscitated, there were no nuns. It has been pointed out that at Ely, unlike other religious houses in the district, there was not complete desolation during the century intervening between the destruction of the former and the construction of the latter house. Some clergy banded themselves together and formed a religious community, of what precise character is not known, but apparently it was something in the nature of a college of secular priests. When the second monastery arose, these clergy were either absorbed or evicted.

Brithnoth (970-981) was the first abbot. He had been Prior of Winchester. He devoted his energies to the consolidation of the new house, securing many fresh endowments, settling the boundaries of the Isle of Ely, and laying out the grounds of the abbey in beautiful order. The church possessed only the bodies of three of the four saints connected with the original foundation. There being no hope of recovering the fourth, Bishop Ethelwold and the abbot resolved to find a substitute in the body of S. Withburga, the youngest sister of S. Etheldreda. Her youth had been spent at Holkham, in Norfolk, where the church is now said to be dedicated to her, and afterwards founded a nunnery at Dereham, in the same county, where she died and was buried. A long account is given by Bentham[61] of the trickery by which her body was purloined and brought to Ely, where it was interred near the bodies of the three abbesses.[62] Brithnoth is said to have been murdered at the instigation of Queen Elfrida, having grievously offended her in many ways, especially by reproving her infamous and abandoned life. This is the same Elfrida who, two years before, had caused her stepson, King Edward (thence called the Martyr), to be assassinated in order that her own son, Ethelred (the Unready), might have the crown. Edward only reigned four years; but during that time much

[60] Introduction to Farren's "Cathedral Cities of Ely and Norwich."

[61] Pages 76-78.

[62] The success of this attempt may have encouraged the monks to make a similar effort some fifty years later. The body of S. Felix, the first of the East Anglian bishops, had been interred at Soham, where he is said to have founded a monastery. Soham was also at first, before the removal of the seat of the bishopric to Dunwich, the headquarters of his diocese. Felix had indeed first been buried at Dunwich, but (probably from fear of the Danes) the body had been removed to Soham. But Soham itself, in its turn, was utterly destroyed by the Danes, and the remains of the bishop became neglected. In 1020 the Abbot of Ramsey obtained permission to move them to his abbey; and while he was doing this, the monks of Ely set out with the intention of intercepting the convoy and securing the body for their own church. A dense fog prevented the Ely men from reaching the monks of Ramsey.

that his father, King Edgar, had done towards establishing the monastic rule in England was set aside. In some instances "the monastic rule was quashed, and minsters dissolved, and monks driven out, and God's servants put down, whom King Edgar had ordered the holy bishop Ethelwold to establish."[63] The queen confessed before her death to having compassed the death of Abbot Brithnoth. His body was conveyed to Ely for interment.

He was succeeded by **Elsin** (981-1016), "of a noble family." In his time very considerable donations and bequests were made to the monastery. In some cases members of the house who rose to eminence and obtained lucrative appointments became benefactors; sometimes the parents of young men who joined the society testified their confidence by munificent gifts; sometimes widows gave manors and lands in their lifetimes or in their wills. In one case at least much wealth was acquired by way of penance. Leofwin, a man of large possessions, in a violent fit of anger had occasioned the death of his own father. In his remorse he betook himself to Rome to obtain absolution, undertaking to perform any penance that might be enjoined. The pope required him to dedicate his eldest son to the religious life in some monastery which he was liberally to endow, and to bestow largely of his substance to the relief of the poor. His son Edelmor was accordingly devoted to the service of God at Ely, and very large estates were assigned by Leofwin to the monastery. He further improved the church, rebuilding and enlarging the south aisle, and joining it to the rest of the building; and in one of its porches, or side-chapels (*in uno portico*), he built an altar to the Virgin Mary, erecting over it a stately image of gold and silver, adorned with valuable jewels. It is probably to this altar that reference is made when we find some speak as if there were a lady-chapel in existence before the present one. At Leofwin's death his body was buried in the church, and to it he bequeathed his entire property.

Alderman Brithnoth, a man of great rank and eminence, and of great reputation as a soldier, was another considerable benefactor. On one occasion he was marching with his forces from the north to encounter the Danes, who had been plundering in Suffolk and had reached Essex. Passing Ramsey Abbey, he sent word to the abbot that he proposed to stop there with his men for refreshment. But the abbot, though willing to entertain the alderman and a few select friends, declined the honour of providing for his troops. This did not suit Brithnoth, and he went on to Ely. There the whole company was hospitably entertained; and Brithnoth was so pleased that he on the next day made over to the monastery a number of manors into their immediate possession, and also assigned certain others, on condition that if he should be slain in battle his body should be buried at Ely. In the battle the English forces were outnumbered, and Brithnoth fell, the Danes taking his head away with them in their triumph. On hearing of his death, the abbot and some of the monks went to the scene of the engagement, recovered the body, and interred it with all honour in their church.

A great accession of dignity was granted by King Ethelred. While his brother, King Edward, was on the throne, Ethelred, with his mother, had visited the tomb of S. Etheldreda, and professed great admiration for her character and work.

---

[63] "Annals of England," i., p. 115.

When Ethelred became king he granted to the churches of Ely, Canterbury, and Glastonbury the office of Chancellor of the King's Court, putting, as it were, the office in commission; so the abbot of each place, or his deputy, officiated as chancellor for periods of four months each. This privilege was only retained till the time of the Normans.

Elsin died in a good old age, "after a life of great sanctity and observance of the commandments of God, and after the acquisition of much honour and great possessions to the church." His death took place, according to the "Liber Eliensis," in King Ethelred's time—that is, not later than 1016. Wharton gives 1019 as the date. Possibly the unsettled state of the kingdom may have caused the abbey to be vacant for three years.

At the Battle of Assendun, 1016, some of the monks of Ely, as well as Ednod, Bishop of Dorchester, and the Abbot of Ramsey, were slain. The Ely monks took with them to the camp the relics of S. Wendreda, which were there lost and never recovered. Canute is thought to have acquired them, and to have bestowed them upon the Church of Canterbury. The body of Bishop Ednod was brought to Ely, with the intention of taking it on to Ramsey, where he had been abbot, for interment. But when the body arrived at Ely it was buried privately by night in the church.

Of **Leofwin**, called also Oschitel (1019?-1022), who is given in the lists as the third abbot, nothing whatever is known, except that he was deposed by the monks, and reinstated, after a journey to Rome, by the pope.

His successor, **Leofric** (1022-1029), who had been prior, is remembered only as being abbot when Archbishop Wulstan of York and Bishop Alfwin of Elmham were buried at Ely, and when divers possessions were acquired by gift or bequest of a certain Countess Godiva.

Leofsin (1029-1045), like his predecessor, was appointed by King Canute. Canute was much in the eastern counties; and he is said to have made a point, when possible, of keeping the Feast of the Purification at Ely, that being the date on which the abbot's turn as chancellor commenced. It was on one of these occasions, while coming by water with his queen and nobles, that the remarkable incident occurred of his hearing the monks singing in the distance, and breaking out himself into verse. Four lines of his song have been preserved.[64] The Latin of them, as given in the "Liber Eliensis," runs thus:

> "Dulce cantaverunt monachi in Ely
> Dum Canutus rex navigaret prope ibi,
> Nunc milites navigate propius ad terram,
> Et simul audiamus monachorum harmoniam."

The incident has attracted many writers, and not a few poems have been written upon it. Wordsworth's sonnet on the subject commences:

---

[64] The Saxon version, together with some valuable notes by Professor Skeat, including a literal transcript, a corrected transcript in the true spelling of the period, and a discussion of the grammatical forms, is given in Dean Stubbs' "Memorials of Ely," pp. 49-52.

"A pleasant music floats along the mere.
From monks in Ely chanting service high,
While as Canute the king is rowing by:
'My oarsmen,' quoth the mighty king, 'draw near,
That we the sweet song of the monks may hear.'"

And in a ballad upon Chelsea, a quarter of New York where the General Theological Seminary of the American church is situated, a poet of that communion has these verses:

"When old Canúte the Dane
Was merry England's king,
A thousand years agone, and more,
As ancient rymours sing,
His boat was rowing down the Ouse,
At eve, one summer day,
Where Ely's tall cathedral peered
Above the glassy way.
Anon, sweet music on his ear,
Comes floating from the fane,
And listening, as with all his soul
Sat old Canúte the Dane;
And reverent did he doff his crown,
To join the clerkly prayer,
While swelled old lauds and litanies
Upon the stilly air."[65]

Ely minster was, however, not a cathedral in Canute's time; and it is a strange poetical licence that can describe an evening just before the Feast of the Purification as a "summer day."

Perhaps the greatest distinction belonging to the monastery at this period was the honour of having educated King Edward the Confessor. He had been brought here in his infancy and offered by his parents on the altar; "and it was a constant tradition with the Monks that he used to take great delight in learning to sing Psalms and godly Hymns, among the children of his own age, in the Cloister, on which account he always retained a favourable regard to the place, after he became King."[66] In 1036, the year after Canute's death, Edward and his brother Alfred came over from Normandy to England, ostensibly to visit their mother, Queen Emma, who lived at Winchester, but really to ascertain the feeling of the nation with regard to the succession to the throne. Alfred fell into the hands of Earl Godwin, by whose orders he was deprived of his eyes and committed to the custody of the monks of Ely. He lived a very short time after this cruel treatment, and died and was buried at Ely.

Abbot **Wilfric** (1045-1065) came from Winchester. He was a kinsman of Ed-

---

[65] "Christian Ballads and Poems," by Rev. Arthur Cleveland Coxe. The author was ultimately Bishop of Western New York.

[66] Bentham, p. 97.

ward the Confessor. Through this relationship, as well as from personal connection with the place, the king greatly favoured the abbey. He granted a confirmatory charter himself, and obtained a bull from the pope confirming all the rights and privileges of the church. But several of the possessions of the abbey were lost in Wilfric's time. In one instance the High Constable of England seized a village belonging to the monks. Proceedings were taken against him and sentence pronounced; but he evaded even the king's orders, and at last actually secured the possession of the village for his own life, after which it was to revert to the true owners. After the Conquest, however, all the lands of this nobleman were seized by the Conqueror, this village among the rest; nor could the Church of Ely ever regain it. In another instance Abbot Wilfric himself was the cause of the loss of much landed property. In order to advance his brother he conveyed to him, without the consent of the monastery, several estates. Upon discovery, the abbot withdrew from Ely in sorrow and disgrace, and soon fell sick and died. As in the previous case, a composition was effected between Guthmund, the late abbot's brother, and the monks, whereby he was to retain the lands for his life. But, as before, these lands were alienated after the Conquest, and never recovered.

Abbot **Thurstan** (1066-1072) was appointed by King Harold, and was the last Saxon abbot. He was a native of the Isle of Ely, having been born at Witchford. He naturally took the part of Edgar Atheling—whom he regarded as the rightful heir after Harold was killed—against William the Conqueror. He gave every support to the many who gathered together in the isle as to a fastness, and encouraged the plans of Hereward. When the cause of the English seemed hopeless, the monks endeavoured to persuade the soldiers to surrender; not being successful, they sent messengers to the king assuring him of their sorrow at having taken part against him, and promising to behave better in future. Afterwards the abbot himself went, and gave the king much information about the place, and the best method of subduing it. But when the isle was finally subdued, the king signified his great displeasure at the behaviour of the monks, and exacted a heavy fine. He is said to have gone in person to the minster, after his victory, and to have made an offering at the altar; but the monks were under such strict surveillance, and the king's visit was so secret, that no one knew of his coming till after he was gone. Thurstan escaped deprivation by his complete submission and prudent conduct, and remained abbot till his death in 1072. But it appears that the monks had not thoroughly made their peace with the Conqueror by the time of Abbot Thurstan's death, for we read, "Eodem anno monachi Elienses, quibusdam Anglorum magnatibus contra regem Willelmum rebellantibus succursum præbentes, exlegati sunt."[67]

He was succeeded by a Norman, **Theodwin** (1072-1075), a monk of Jumièges. This was a Benedictine abbey of great repute in the diocese of Rouen. Its church had been built during the abbacy of Robert, afterwards Archbishop of Canterbury; and he died and was buried at Jumièges. Theodwin was present at the Council of London in 1075. He died the same year.

For upwards of six years the affairs of the monastery were administered by Godfrey, one of the monks. He was an able and efficient administrator. In his time

[67] "Chronicon Angliæ Petriburgense," p. 57, *sub anno* 1072.

the king sent a number of knights and gentlemen to live at Ely, and he supported them out of the revenues of the house. The names and armorial bearings of these pensioners are preserved in a curious painting called the "Tabula Eliensis," now in the palace. This is a copy, as it is said, of one formerly in the refectory. It cannot be earlier than the fifteenth century. There are in it forty compartments, in each of which is represented a knight and a monk, the names of both being given above, and the arms of the knights being placed beside their heads. Some of the names are still to be found among the nobility and gentry of England, and in some instances the very same armorial bearings are used. This is the case in the families of Lacy, St. Leger, Montfort, Clare, Touchet, Furnival, Fulke, Newbury, Lucy, Talbot, Fitzallen, Longchamp. It need hardly be pointed out that no contemporary Norman painting could have given such shields of arms to the different knights, heraldry having only established itself as a science in England in the thirteenth century.

The affairs of the abbey had been in a very unsettled state since the time when the Camp of Refuge was attacked, so many of the estates of the church having been granted to Norman followers of the Conqueror. But the king's resentment at last gave way, and he was induced to sanction an inquiry into the rights and liberties of the monastery. He appointed his brother Odo, then Bishop of Bayeux, to summon an assembly of barons, sheriffs, and others interested in the matter, to consider and determine the claims of the monks. The meeting was held at Kentford, in Suffolk; and the report was so favourable that the king directed the church to be put into possession of all the rights, customs, and privileges which it enjoyed at the time of King Edward's death.

Godfrey, the administrator, being made Abbot of Malmesbury, an abbot was at length given to Ely in the person of **Simeon** (1081-1093). He was prior of Winchester, and brother to Walkelin, Bishop of Winchester. He was very old when he came to Ely; but though upwards of eighty-six years of age at the time, he remained abbot for more than twelve years. He laid the foundations of the present church, and completed some part of the building, as has been previously told. He died in 1093.[68]

King William II. immediately took possession of the abbey estates, let them to various tenants, and appointed a receiver to pay the rents into his treasury. This arrangement lasted during the remainder of his reign.

King Henry I., upon coming to the throne, at once "restored the liberties" of the church, and made Richard (1100-1107) abbot. He was a Norman and a kinsman of the king, as his grandfather, Earl Gilbert, was descended from Robert, Duke of Normandy. He successfully resisted the claim of the Bishop of Lincoln to give him benediction, though Simeon had received benediction from Bishop Remigius. In the Council of London, in 1102, Abbot Richard, with many others, was deposed. "Anselmus archiepiscopus, concilio convocato apud Londiniam, rege consentiente, plures deposuit abbates vel propter simoniam vel propter aliam vitæ infa-

---

[68] Bentham says, "after he had lived too years complete." The "Liber Eliensis" says he was in his eighty-seventh year when appointed abbot; if so, he was nearly, but not quite, one hundred years old at his death.

miam."[69] The abbots of Burgh, Ramsey, and Ely were three of nine so deposed. The "Liber Eliensis" attributes Richard's deposition to the intrigues of the Court. The pope annulled the sentence in the following year. This abbot proceeded with the building of the church, and seems to have finished the Norman transepts and choir, and perhaps the whole of the Norman tower. He is, however, most worthy of note from having been the first to suggest the creation of the See of Ely. He submitted the idea to the king, who was quite favourable; and he then sent messengers to the pope to obtain his approval. Before this could be secured the abbot died, but in little more than two years after his death the proposal was carried into effect.

Richard was the last of the ten abbots. Hervey, Bishop of Bangor, had the management of the affairs of the abbey for the next two years. His rigorous discipline at Bangor had aroused very violent opposition, which came at last to armed insurrection, and the bishop had withdrawn to the king's court for safety. When appointed administrator of the abbey at Ely, he exerted himself to bring to a successful conclusion the creation of the bishopric. The consent of the Bishop of Lincoln to the subdivision of his diocese was secured by a grant of the Manor of Spaldwick. At a Council of London in 1108 the enormous size of the Lincoln diocese was under consideration; and Ely seemed on every account to be the best place for the cathedral of a new diocese to be taken from it. The pope was entirely favourable to the design. Though the letters announcing the pope's consent were dated November 21st, 1108, it was not till October, 1109, that the king granted his charter for constituting the bishopric. In this he nominated Hervey to be the first bishop, in accordance with the recommendation of the pope himself.

The monastery did not come to an end by the substitution of a bishop for an abbot. But for the purposes of this handbook, concerned as it is mainly with the fabric of the cathedral, the remainder of the historical portion will be associated with the names of the bishops—not that, by any means, the most important works connected with the church were due to the initiation of the bishops, nor was the cost always, or indeed generally, defrayed by them. The monastic body spent large sums upon the building, as has been seen in the case of the octagon: but these works are mostly to be credited to the whole body, and, except in a few cases, which are duly noticed, are not assigned specially to the prior who was the head of the house at the time.

---

[69] "Chronicon Angliæ Petriburgense," *sub anno* 1102.

BISHOP ALCOCK'S CHANTRY FROM THE RETRO-CHOIR

CHAPTER V.

HISTORY OF THE SEE.

Ely thus became a cathedral—of the kind that was called conventual cathedrals. No such cathedral had a dean and canons till the time of Henry VIII. The prior and convent were the custodians of the fabric, and perhaps to a certain extent they acted as the bishop's council; and the bishop, as representing the abbot, had the right to preside in the chapter-house whenever he chose.[70] The bishop also had the power of appointing several of the officers of the monastery, and of displacing them. At Ely the priors were appointed by the bishop until 1198. In 1197 the offices of bishop and prior were vacant at the same time, and the convent was unable to elect a bishop without having a prior: so the Archbishop of Canterbury authorised the monks to proceed to the election of a prior; and it is believed that subsequent priors were all elected by the monks, and not appointed by the bishop.

The first bishop, as has been seen, was **Hervey** (1109-1131), Bishop of Bangor.[71] He had been consecrated in 1102. His ecclesiastical discipline in Wales was very strict, and he made many enemies; and he thought to carry out his spiritual censures with the help of armed forces, but insurrections arose, in one of which his own brother and several of his company were slain. Upon this Bishop Hervey made his way to the English court, where he remained until he was sent to take charge of Ely monastery at the death of Abbot Richard. He was bishop here for nearly twenty-two years, and was most active and painstaking in managing the very difficult business of settling the affairs of the bishopric and monastery in such a way that justice was done to both. He died in 1131.

After two years **Nigel** (1133-1169) was made bishop. He was Prebendary of S. Paul's and also Treasurer to King Henry I. This latter office necessitated his continuous absence from his diocese, and may also serve to explain the very active part he took in the civil wars. He espoused the cause of the Empress Matilda, and built a castle at Ely as a military position where a good stand could be made against the partisans of Stephen. More than once he narrowly escaped being taken; and when

---

[70] Cathedrals "of the old foundation" were cathedrals from the first, and had deans and chapters of secular canons. Those that were once conventual churches had no deans or canons till Henry VIII. An easy way of identifying cathedrals of the old foundation is this: if the non-resident canons have the title of prebendaries, they are members of a cathedral of the old foundation. The modern dignity of honorary canon was created in order that all other cathedrals might have a body of clergy corresponding to the prebendaries of the ancient cathedrals.

[71] He is called, in Bishop Stubbs' "Registrum Sacrum Anglicanum," Herve le Breton.

at first Stephen's cause prospered, all Bishop Nigel's estates and property were seized. When the chances of war favoured Matilda he recovered the Isle of Ely and was fully restored to his bishopric. By this time he had had enough of fighting, and made his peace with Stephen. But his troubles were not at an end. As he was going to consult some friends who were with the Empress upon a matter unconnected with politics, he was nearly taken prisoner by a party of the king's forces, losing all his baggage and everything he had with him. Being summoned to Rome, he was, in his absence, suspected of favouring the king's enemies, and his possessions were again seized. Only with great difficulty, and after paying a large fine, did he obtain Stephen's pardon. At one time he was suspended by the Pope "pro bonis Ecclesise suse dispersis"; but the suspension was removed on condition that he restored the goods. When King Henry II. came to the throne, Nigel was made Baron of the Exchequer. Some have attributed to him the foundation of the hospital for canons regular dedicated to S. John at Cambridge, an institution afterwards absorbed in Lady Margaret's College of S. John the Evangelist. He died in 1169.

There was an interval of four years before a new bishop was appointed, and it was more than five before **Geoffrey Riddell** (1174-1189) was consecrated. He was one of the king's chaplains, a Baron of the Exchequer, and Archdeacon of Canterbury. The delay in his consecration was due to a disagreement between King Henry II. and his son Henry, who had actually been crowned, the latter considering that he ought to have a voice in the appointment. The dispute was not settled without an appeal to Rome. Bishop Riddell furthered the building of the church, and embellished it in various ways. He also recovered some property that had been taken away. Before consecration he had been compelled to profess publicly that he had had nothing to do with the murder of Archbishop Becket: "Mortem S. Thomæ Archiepiscopi neque verbo neque facto neque scripto scienter procuravit." He became very wealthy. He died in 1189 at Winchester, whither he had gone to welcome King Richard. Not long after his death his tomb was violated, and the episcopal ring on his finger purloined. The violators were anathematised from the pulpit.

The fourth bishop was **William Longchamp** (1189-1197), Chancellor of England and subsequently Papal Legate. When the king went abroad he was appointed to govern England south of the Trent. He behaved in this office "with great insolence, pride, and oppression," and having particularly offended John, the king's brother, he made an attempt to escape from the country in the disguise of a woman; but he was detected at Dover and thrown into prison. Being allowed, after a time, to go to Normandy, he there waited until the king's return, by whom he was restored to favour. He died in 1197 at Poictiers, and was buried there in a Cistercian abbey, his heart being brought to Ely.

He was succeeded by **Eustace** (1198-1215), Archdeacon of Richmond, Treasurer of York, Dean of Salisbury, and Keeper of the Great Seal. He was one of the bishops to whom was entrusted the invidious employment of publishing the excommunication of King John and putting the kingdom under an interdict. For this, in 1209, he was outlawed, and had to leave the country. Upon the king's submission in 1213, he (with Archbishop Stephen Langton and three other bishops) returned to England. He built the galilee at the west end of the church. He died in 1215 at Reading.

Robert of York was chosen by the monks to succeed him. They had at first selected Geoffrey de Burgh, but for some reason that does not appear they altered their minds before making their selection known. Robert got possession of the temporalities, and even gave away preferments that were in the bishop's gift, for five years; but the king never consented to his appointment, nor was he ever consecrated. He took the part of the French against the king, who at last applied to the pope to nominate some one else to the See of Ely. Accordingly, upon the recommendation of the Archbishop of Canterbury, the Legate Pandulph, and the Bishop of Salisbury, who had been authorised by the pope to make the selection, **John Pherd** (1220-1225), Abbot of Fountains, hence called De Fontibus, was made bishop. He was also Treasurer of England. He died at Downham in 1225, and was succeeded by the same **Geoffrey De Burgh** (1225-1228) who had at first been elected by the convent upon the death of Eustace. He was Archdeacon of Norwich, and brother to Hubert de Burgh, Earl of Kent. He gave much costly plate to the monastery, as well as three hundred acres of land.

Upon his death, **Hugh Norwold** or Northwold (1229-1254), Abbot of Bury S. Edmunds, became bishop. He had been a justice itinerant. He was one of the embassy sent to conduct to England the king's bride, Eleanor of Provençe. "He was one of the most eminent examples of piety and virtue in his time." He is especially commended for his hospitality and liberality to the poor; and he was a great benefactor to the monastery. He spent more than £5000 on the fabric of the church, and built the palace. The six eastern bays of the presbytery are his work. After removing to this new part of the church the remains of the three sainted abbesses and S. Withburga and also the so-called relics of S. Alban, he dedicated the whole church on September 17th, 1252, in the presence of King Henry III. and his son, Prince Edward. Bishop Norwold died at Downham in 1254, and was buried at the feet of S. Etheldreda, where a splendid monument was erected over his body, now removed to the north side of the presbytery, beneath the third arch from the east.

The next bishop was **William De Kilkenny** (1255-1256), Archdeacon of Coventry and chancellor of the king. After his consecration, which took place ten months after his election, he only lived thirteen months. He was consecrated by Archbishop Boniface at Belley, in Savoy, a place near the Rhone, about forty miles east of Lyons. He died in Spain while negotiating a treaty, and was there buried, at Sugho. His heart was brought to Ely.

Hugh Belsham (1257-1286) the sub-prior, came next. He founded Peterhouse (now S. Peter's College) at Cambridge. He had been elected in defiance of the king's recommendation, and the king tried to annul his election; but he proceeded to Rome, and was actually consecrated there by the pope. It is in connection with his election that we learn that the custom of the monks was to depute the election of a bishop to a committee of seven chosen from among themselves. Bishop Hugh died at Doddington in 1286.

The next bishop, **John Kirkby** (1286-1290), although at the time of his appointment Dean of Wimborne, Archdeacon of York, and Canon both of Wells and York, was only in deacon's orders. He was accordingly ordained priest one day and consecrated bishop the next. Three years previously he had been elected to the See of Rochester, but had declined it. He had also been Chancellor and Treasurer of England. He gave to his successors a house in Holborn, which formed the nucleus of the grand palace afterwards erected, adjacent property being subsequently acquired. He died in 1290.

His successor, **William De Louth** (1290-1298) was not even in holy orders at all when elected; yet he held prebends at S. Paul's, York, and Lincoln, the Archdeaconry of Durham, and the Deanery of S. Martin's-le-Grand. He is the only Bishop of Ely who was consecrated at Ely (it was in S. Mary's Church, not the cathedral), a provincial council of bishops happening to meet there at the time.

Ralph Walpole (1299-1302), Bishop of Norwich, was, on the death of Bishop Louth in 1298, translated to Ely; the prior, John Salmon, who had been elected by the monks, being made instead Bishop of Norwich. Walpole had been formerly Archdeacon of Ely. He revised the statutes of the monastery during the short time that he held the see, which was less than three years.

The next bishop, **Robert Orford** (1302-1310), like his predecessor, Hugh Belsham, was consecrated at Rome, though not, as he had been, by the pope himself. The Archbishop of Canterbury had refused his consent to the appointment on the ground that the elect was illiterate, but the pope overruled the objection. He died at Downham in 1310.

A monk of the house, **John Keeton** (1310-1316), succeeded. King Edward II. visited Ely in his time, and while there settled the controversy between Ely and S. Albans as to the true place where the body of the proto-martyr of England was deposited. The remains of S. Alban had been carried off to Denmark by the Danes, after plundering the abbey raised to his honour, and recovered by a trick. At a later time, fearing again an attack from the Danes, the Abbot of S. Albans sent to Ely a chest containing (so he said) the relics of the martyr for safe custody. When the troubles were over, the monks of Ely sent back the chest, but with other bones in it, supposing that they had thereby secured the true relics for their own church. So the Abbot of S. Albans declared that they were not the true relics that he had sent to Ely, but that he had buried them in a fresh place in his own church. The king, in 1314, decided the matter in favour of S. Albans.

At the death of Bishop Keeton in 1316 the bishopric was conferred upon **John Hotham** (1316-1337), Chancellor of the Exchequer. Bentham calls him Prebendary of York and Rector of Collingham; Browne Willis calls him Provost of Queen's College, Oxford, and Chancellor of the University, and S.T.P., being the first bishop in his list who is credited with any university degree. He was a man of great eminence both as a bishop and as a statesman. In his political capacity he was Lord Chancellor. He was employed more than once on foreign embassies. He was one of the commissioners to arrange a truce between England and Scotland after the Battle of Myton in 1319, at which he had been present. He was made special commissioner to settle the troubles in Gascony. In his ecclesiastical capacity he added much landed property both to the see and the monastery. He erected the choir, providing for the building of the western bays after the fall of the tower. He obtained confirmatory charters from the king, and also a grant giving to the prior and convent the custody of the temporalities of the see during a vacancy, upon paying to the king, as long as their custody lasted, at the rate of £2000 a year. He died, "vir prudens, Justus, et munificus," in 1337.

The monks desired that their prior, John Crauden, should become bishop; but the king translated hither **Simon Montacute** (1337-1345), Bishop of Worcester. In a letter to the pope about him, in 1318, King Edward II. calls him his cousin (*consanguineus*). He materially assisted the buildings at the church, particularly the lady-chapel. He died in 1345.

Again the nomination of the monks, in favour of their prior, Alan de Walsingham, was set aside, and **Thomas De Lisle** (1345-1361) became bishop. He was prior of the Dominican Friars at Winchester. For nearly the whole of his episcopate he was engaged in a prolonged controversy with Lady Blanche Wake, a daughter of the Earl of Lancaster—the same lady who afterwards married John of Gaunt and became mother of King Henry IV. Her estates were contiguous to the bishop's manors in Huntingdonshire, and frequent disputes arose about their boundaries. The tenants took violent measures to assert the claims of their respective landlords, and much litigation ensued. The bishop, by his haughty behaviour, offended both the courts and the king, to whom he appealed; and at last he was constrained to escape to Avignon, then the seat of the pope. Here he had been consecrated; and here, while negotiations were proceeding for settling the dispute, in 1361 he died; and here he was buried.

This time the monks elected, not one of their own body, but the Dean of Lichfield. But once again their nomination was disregarded, and #Simon Langham# (1362-1366) was appointed bishop. He was Abbot of Westminster and Treasurer of England. He had lately declined the See of London. He was afterwards Lord Chancellor, and in 1366 he was translated to Canterbury; but he only remained archbishop till he was created a cardinal in 1368. In 1374 he was appointed Bishop of Præneste. Like his predecessor, he died and was buried at Avignon. This was in 1376. After three years his body was removed to Westminster Abbey, where his handsome monument is well known. The inscription implies that all the world sorrowed at his death: "Orbe dolente Pater ... ruit."

On his removal to Canterbury, the Bishop of Bath and Wells, **John Barnet** (1366-1373), was translated to Ely. He had been previously Bishop of Worcester, and for a time Treasurer of England. He "beautified" five of the windows in the presbytery. He died at Hatfield in 1373, but was buried at Ely.

His successor was **Thomas Fitz-Alan** (1374-1388), son of the Earl of Arundel, Archdeacon of Taunton. He is said at the time not to have been in holy orders and under twenty-three years of age. The convent had in vain elected the Archdeacon of Northampton. Bishop Arundel (so he is generally called) was Chancellor of England in 1386, but resigned that office in 1389, the year after he was made Archbishop of York. He ultimately became Archbishop of Canterbury, and died in 1414. He almost rebuilt the Bishop of Ely's palace in London. He fell into disfavour with King Richard II., and was banished; but he returned to England on the accession of King Henry IV. He was buried at Canterbury.

John Fordham (1388-1425), who succeeded Bishop Arundel at Ely, was Bishop of Durham. He had been Keeper of the Privy Seal. He died at Downham in 1425, and was followed by **Philip Morgan** (1426-1435), Bishop of Worcester. The king had given licence to the monks to elect, and had recommended his confessor. They elected instead their prior; but neither obtained the see. In Bishop Morgan's time the University of Cambridge secured entire freedom from the ecclesiastical jurisdiction of the Bishops of Ely: in the time of the previous bishop the University had got rid of the necessity of presenting their chancellor to the Bishop of Ely for confirmation. Bishop Morgan died at Hatfield in 1435, and was buried at the Charterhouse in London.

There was much dispute about the next bishop. The monks chose Fitz-Hugh, Bishop of London; but he died. The king then recommended the Bishop of S. David's; but the monks preferred Thomas Bouchier, Bishop of Worcester, whom the king refused. Bouchier appealed to the pope, who at first confirmed his election; but the bishop-elect was afraid to present the papal bull. This was an opportunity for the king (Henry VI.) "to gratify one of his numerous adherents of the French nation, who had lost their all in that kingdom, and followed his fortunes in this." He accordingly obtained the pope's consent to appoint #Lewis De Luxemburg# (1438-1443), Archbishop of Rouen, to be administrator of the Diocese of Ely, at the same time assigning him the £2000 a year due from the prior and convent to the king during a vacancy. The bulls for Bishop Bouchier's translation from Worcester were revoked. This was in 1438, which is held to be the beginning of Bishop Luxemburg's tenure of the see; but the spiritualities were not legally surrendered to him till the next year, and even then it seems to have been only under the title of "Perpetual Administrator of the See of Ely"; and in formal documents some time later he still has the same title, and even in the pope's bull appointing a new Bishop of Ely after his death. He had been Bishop of Terouanne, Chancellor of Normandy, and Governor of Paris, and was a great upholder in France of the cause of the King of England. He was afterwards cardinal. He was hardly ever in his diocese of Ely. He died at Hatfield in 1443, and was buried at Ely, his heart being taken to Normandy to be interred at Rouen.

There was now no opposition to the appointment of **Thomas Bouchier** (1444-1454), Bishop of Worcester. He was of the blood royal, being grandson of Thomas of Woodstock, Duke of Gloucester, son of King Edward III. He was not liked at Ely, where, after his installation, he would never take part in any solemn service. He became Archbishop of Canterbury in 1454, Lord Chancellor in 1455, and cardinal in 1464. He crowned three kings. He died in 1486 at his palace at Knole, and was buried at Canterbury.

He was succeeded by **William Gray** (1454-1478), Archdeacon of Northampton. He was for a time Treasurer of England and employed as Commissioner and Ambassador. He gave material assistance to the cost of the works at the west tower of the cathedral, and in various ways improved the presbytery. He was a great benefactor to Balliol College, Oxford. He died at Downham in 1478.

The next bishop was **John Morton** (1479-1486). He had held very numerous preferments, including no less than five archdeaconries, and was Master of the Rolls. He was made Lord Chancellor in the same year that he was appointed to Ely. While bishop he executed some important works to improve the navigation and drainage of the fens. The great artificial cut between Peterborough and Wisbech which he constructed is still called Morton's Learn. He became Archbishop of Canterbury in 1486, and cardinal in 1493. He died at Knole in 1500, and was buried at Canterbury.

THE NORTH CHOIR AISLE, LOOKING EAST.

Photochrom Co. Ltd. Photo.

John Alcock (1486-1500) succeeded him at Ely. He was Bishop of Worcester, previously of Rochester, and had been for a few months Lord Chancellor. He founded Jesus College, Cambridge, upon the dissolution of the ancient nunnery of S. Rhadegund. He was a great architect, and erected many costly buildings. He built the great hall in the palace at Ely, much improved the palace at Downham, founded a school at Hull, and erected a chapel in the church there, and built the beautiful chapel in Ely Cathedral, where his body now lies. He died at Wisbech in 1500.

After nearly a year's interval, **Richard Redman** (1501-1505) became bishop. He was Bishop of Exeter, previously of S. Asaph. He died at Ely House in London in 1505.

BISHOP WEST'S CHAPEL.

Photochrom Co. Ltd. Photo.

The next bishop was **James Stanley** (1506-1515), son of the first Earl of Derby. Among other preferments he held was the Wardenship of Manchester. He built part of Somersham palace, and was a considerable benefactor to the Collegiate Church of Manchester, where he was ultimately buried, although he left directions in his will to be buried at Ely. His numerous promotions are possibly due to the influence of his stepmother, the famous Lady Margaret, Countess of Richmond and Derby, the mother of King Henry VII. He was very little at Ely, and bore an indifferent moral character. The quaint set of verses[72] drawing his character says there was "little Priest's metal in him," that he was "a goodly tall man as any in England," that he was made bishop "for his wisdom and parentage," that he was "a great Viander as any in his days," which last expression probably means that he was unduly given to hospitality. He died at Manchester in 1515.

Nicholas West (1515-1533) who succeeded him, was the son of a baker. He had been employed in foreign embassies, and was Dean of Windsor and Archdeacon of Derby. He lived in great splendour, and relieved the poor with much bounty. He was a benefactor to King's College, Cambridge, where he had been fellow. He took the part of Queen Katherine of Arragon, to whom he was chaplain, in the question of the divorce; and the disfavour into which he consequently fell with the king is thought to have hastened his death, which took place in 1533.

THE BRASS OF BISHOP GOODRICH, LORD CHANCELLOR TO EDWARD
VI., DIED 1554.

(He holds the Great Seal in his right hand.)

____

[72] Quoted by Bentham, p. 187.

Thomas Goodrich (1533-1554) was a "zealous forwarder of the Reformation." He was one of the revisers of the translation of the New Testament, and assisted in the compilation of the Prayer-book. He was also Lord Chancellor. In his time, in 1539, the monastery was surrendered to the king. All the inmates were pensioned or otherwise provided for. Dugdale gives the revenues of the monastery at its dissolution as £1084 6*s.* 9*d.*; Speed says £1301 8*s.* 2*d.* Bishop Goodrich's monumental brass in the cathedral is a very important example of such memorials. He died at Somersham in 1554.

Thomas Thirlby (1554-1559) was Bishop of Norwich, having been previously the first and only Bishop of Westminster. "He is said to have been a discreet moderate man"; but he lived in troublous times, and had the distasteful task of committing some so-called heretics to the flames. He was dispossessed of his bishopric soon after the accession of Queen Elizabeth, and sent to the Tower. He was, however, soon released, and permitted to live in retirement with Archbishop Parker at Lambeth, where he died and was buried in 1570.

Richard Cox (1559-1581) was Dean of Westminster and of Christ Church, Oxford. He was much troubled at the series of alienations of the property of the see insisted upon by the Government, and used every effort to secure what he could for his successors; and for this opposition, and also for his being married, he fell under the queen's disfavour, and many times solicited permission to resign his see, but he remained bishop till his death in 1581.

For eighteen years the see was vacant, all the revenues being absorbed by the Crown. At last **Martin Heaton** (1600-1609) was made bishop. He was Dean of Winchester. He has the reputation of having been a pious, hospitable man, and a good preacher. He died at Mildenhall, in Suffolk, in 1609.

His successor was the famous **Lancelot Andrewes** (1609-1619), Bishop of Chichester. He was a man "of extraordinary endowments, very pious and charitable, of a most blameless life, an eminent Preacher, of universal learning, and one of those principally concerned in the new Translation of the Bible." He became Bishop of Winchester in 1619, and died in 1626, being buried at S. Saviour's, Southwark. Milton has a Latin elegy upon his death, written when the poet was in his seventeenth year. Dean Duport[73] has also a short poem in the form of an epitaph on him, in which occur these lines:

> "Hoc sub nomine quippe continentur
> Virtus, ingenium, eruditioque,
> Fides, et pietas, amorque veri,
> Doctrinæ jubar, Orthodoxiæque
> Ingens destina, schismatis flagellum,
> Tortor tortilis illius Draconis,
> Scutum Ecclesiæ et ensis Anglicanæ
> Contra bella, minas, et arma Romæ."

Nicolas Felton (1619-1626) was Bishop of Bristol. He died in 1626, and was buried at S. Antholin's, London, where he had been rector.

[73] Of Peterborough, in his "Musæ Subsecivæ."

John Buckridge (1628-1631) succeeded after an interval of eighteen months. He was Bishop of Rochester. "A Person of great Learning and Worth, and a true Son of the Church of England." He died in 1631, and was buried at Bromley in Kent, near the palace of the Bishops of Rochester.

Francis White (1631-1638) was Bishop of Norwich, previously of Carlisle. Dying in 1638, he was buried in S. Paul's Cathedral.

Matthew Wren (1638-1667) was also Bishop of Norwich, and previously of Hereford. He was an unflinching supporter of King Charles I. and Archbishop Laud, and had a full share of the sufferings which his principles involved, being imprisoned in the Tower for eighteen years, from which imprisonment he was only released at the Restoration, when of course he was restored to his see. Sir Christopher Wren was his nephew. He had been fellow of Pembroke, Cambridge, and after the Restoration he built a chapel for his old college, in which he was buried upon his death in 1667.

Benjamin Laney (1667-1675) had been Bishop of Peterborough and then of Lincoln. He spent a great deal of money in repairing the palace at Ely, which was much dilapidated. He died in 1675. He is described on his monument as being "facundia amabilis, acumine terribilis, eruditione auctissimus."

Peter Gunning (1675-1684) had been Regius Professor of Divinity at Cambridge, Master of Corpus Christi, and then of S. John's College, and Bishop of Chichester. He composed the prayer "For all Sorts and Conditions of Men" in the Prayer-book. He is very highly praised in the inscription on his monument, which also records that he never was married.

Francis Turner (1685-1691) had been Master of S. John's College, Cambridge, also Dean of Windsor and Bishop of Rochester. He was, with six other bishops, sent to the Tower in 1688 for presenting to the king a petition which was called a seditious libel. They were committed on June 8th and tried on June 29th. Amidst universal acclamations of joy and enthusiasm they were acquitted. In 1691 Bishop Turner, with Archbishop Sancroft and four other bishops, upon refusing to take the oaths to William and Mary, were deprived of their bishoprics. He lived in retirement for nine years, and died in 1700. He was buried at Therfield, in Hertfordshire, where he had been rector.

Simon Patrick (1691-1707) had been Dean of Peterborough and Bishop of Chichester. He was a very learned man and a great writer. His writings, says his epitaph, are superior to any inscription and more lasting than any marble. He died in 1707.

John Moore (1707-1714), Bishop of Norwich, was a book-collector, and after his death his library was purchased by the king and presented to the University of Cambridge. He died in 1714.

William Fleetwood (1714-1723) was translated to Ely from S. Asaph. He was a great supporter of the principles of the Revolution, and towards the end of Queen Anne's reign, when the Jacobites seemed to be making very many adherents, he published some sermons, to which was prefixed a preface setting forth his opinion of the dangerous tendency of the views that were being spread so industriously. The House of Commons condemned the book; but upon the arrival of King George, his services were recognised by his translation to Ely. He died at Tottenham in 1723.

Thomas Greene (1723-1738) was Bishop of Norwich and previously Master of Corpus Christi College, Cambridge. In Masters' history of that college a very high character of him is given, and his publications are greatly praised. He was zealous "for the Protestant Succession in the illustrious House of Hanover." He died at Ely House in London in 1738. His epitaph in the cathedral says he had the credit of diligence, impartiality, and integrity in the administration of his diocese. One expression is curious: "Pietate et Annis gravis, Accepta tandem Rude, Uxori et numerosæ Proli ... Flebilis decessit." According to this he was greatly lamented "when he received his discharge."

Robert Butts (1738-1748), like his predecessor, came from Norwich, where he had been dean and then bishop. He died at Ely House in 1748, possessed (according to the epitaph at Ely) of nearly all the virtues. He came of a gentle family of moderate means: "tenui vico, at honesto genere."

Again a Bishop of Norwich was translated to Ely. **Sir Thomas Gooch**, second Baronet of Benacre (1748-1754), had been Master of Caius College, Cambridge, and Bishop of Bristol before he went to Norwich. At Cambridge he was instrumental in raising funds for building the Senate House; at Norwich he greatly improved the palace, and obtained charters for two societies for the relief of widows and orphans of the clergy; but there is no record of anything special achieved by him at Ely. He died at Ely House in 1754, and was buried in the chapel at Caius, where is a lengthy inscription enumerating his preferments and his three wives.

Matthias Mawson (1754-1770) had been Master of Corpus Christi College, Cambridge, Bishop of Llandaff, and Bishop of Chichester. While at Ely he spent large sums on the cathedral alterations, as described above, and was also very active in encouraging, by his advice and purse, the steps that were being taken to improve the roads near Ely and to erect draining-mills. The adjoining lowlands had "been several years under water; and the publick roads, at the same time, in so bad a state, as not to be travelled with safety."[74] He founded several scholarships at his old college, of the aggregate value of £400 a year. He died in 1770.

Edmund Keene (1771-1781) had been Master of Peterhouse and Bishop of Chester. The inscription on his monument at Ely was written by himself. He died in 1781.

The Hon. James Yorke (1781-1808), fifth son of the first Earl of Hardwicke, had been Dean of Lincoln, Bishop of S. David's, and Bishop of Gloucester. He died in 1808, and was buried at Forthampton, in Gloucestershire.

Thomas Dampier (1808-1812) was son of the Dean of Durham. He was Dean and afterwards Bishop of Rochester. He died suddenly in London in 1812, and was buried in the chapel of Eton College.

---

[74] Bentham, p. 213.

BISHOP WOODFORD'S TOMB.

Photochrom Co. Ltd. Photo.

Bowyer Edward Sparke (1812-1836), Bishop of Chester, previously Dean of Bristol. In his time the temporal jurisdiction of the bishop over the Isle of Ely came to an end. On State occasions a sword used to be carried before the bishop when he attended cathedral service; but this practice ceased when it was no longer right to exhibit any emblem of judicial authority. The sword itself was buried with Bishop Sparke.

Joseph Allen (1836-1845), Bishop of Bristol. He published some sermons and charges. He secured from the ecclesiastical commissioners a large increase in the income of the bishopric.

Thomas Turton (1845-1864) had been Regius Professor of Divinity at Cambridge, Dean of Peterborough, and, for a short time, Dean of Westminster. He was author of several works. By his will he left £500 for the improvement of the nave of the cathedral. He died in 1864.

Edward Harold Browne (1864-1873) was of great reputation as a scholar and theologian. He was chairman of the Old Testament Revision Committee. He became Bishop of Winchester in 1873, and died at Bitterne, in Hampshire, in 1891. He was buried at West End, Southampton.

James Russell Woodford (1873-1885) was Vicar of Leeds. He published many sermons and lectures, and was well known as a successful organizer and an eloquent preacher. He died in 1885.

Lord Alwyne Compton (1885-1905) was a son of the second Marquess of Northampton, and was previously Dean of Worcester. Resigned, and died, 1906, and was buried at S. Martin's, Canterbury.

Frederic Henry Chase (1905-) was formerly Norrisian and Lady Margaret Professor, and President of Queens' College, Cambridge, and is the author of numerous works in critical theology.

The names and dates of the earlier bishops are taken from Bishop Stubbs' "Registrum Sacrum Anglicanum." Of the bishops between 1609 and 1845 there was only one (Peter Gunning) who was not translated to Ely from some other see. It is now an unwritten law that the Bishop of Ely should be a Cambridge man. For at least two centuries and a half this rule has been followed, if we except Francis Turner; and he, though of New College, Oxford, had been Master of S. John's, Cambridge. Unless otherwise stated, the bishops were buried at Ely.

The original diocese of Ely was enlarged, in 1837, by the addition of the counties of Huntingdon and Bedford, and the archdeaconry of Sudbury.

PRIOR CRAUDEN'S CHAPEL.

Photochrom Co. Ltd. Photo.

CHAPTER VI.

THE PRECINCTS.

Besides numerous remains of mediæval architecture to be found in the residences and private grounds of the cathedral clergy, there are some buildings of great interest to the south of the cathedral, the two most remarkable being the infirmary and Prior Crauden's chapel. Of the former no more than the piers and arches are to be seen, as the roof is gone, and the whole has been converted into residences. The latter is quite perfect.

THE INFIRMARY

The **Infirmary** is in the same relative position to the church as at Peterborough, at the south-east. The plan was that of an ordinary church, with nave, aisles, and chancel; but the chancel was the chapel, the aisles were the quarters of the inmates, and the nave was a common hall, or ambulatory. So complete was the resemblance to a church that the true purpose of this and other similar buildings elsewhere had been quite forgotten, and it was left to Professor Willis to discover that the remains were not those of a disused church. Bentham[75] has an engraving of the arches and clerestory, divested of all the domestic additions, which to a modern

[75] "History," 1771, Plate IV.

student of ecclesiastical architecture indicates at once a building of Norman date, which is described as an elevation "of the remains of the Old Conventual Church of Ely, built in the time of the Heptarchy, A.D. 673, and repaired in King Edgar's Reign, A.D. 970." In the plan given in the same plate an imaginary apse is marked out with dotted lines.[76] In the chapel is a groined roof, and this belongs to the latter part of the twelfth century; but the nave arches, where are some very good and unusual mouldings, have nothing of Transitional work, and in the absence of documentary evidence would be assigned to 1140 or 1150. The hall, situated to the north of what would, in a church, be called the north aisle of the nave, is the work of Walsingham.

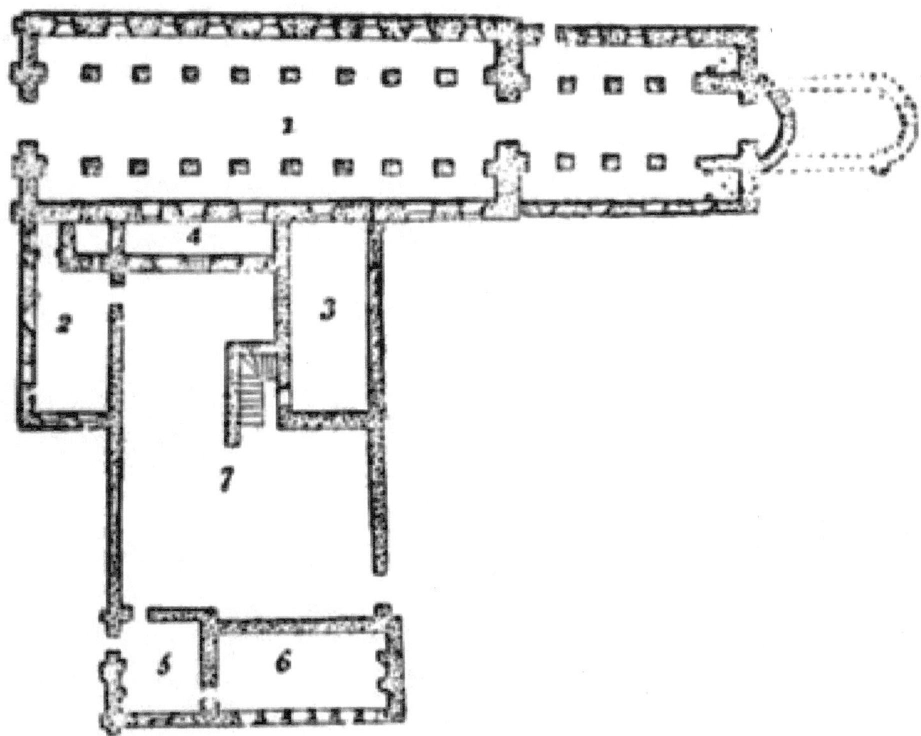

PLAN OF THE INFIRMARY AS GIVEN IN BENTHAM;S "HISTORY AND ANTIQUITIES."

PRIOR CRAUDEN'S CHAPEL

Prior Crauden's Chapel is a most exquisite specimen of the Decorated period, designed by the same master mind that created the octagon and the lady-chapel. Crauden was prior from 1321 to 1341. Built as a private chapel, it was at one time

[76] Another instance of imperfect acquaintance with church architecture is found in one plan of the cathedral (not in Bentham) in which the lady-chapel is called the chapter-house.

converted into a dwelling, but is now restored to sacred uses as the chapel of the King's School. It is situated to the south of the deanery. It is of small dimensions, being only thirty-one feet long; and this is exactly double its breadth. The vaulted roof springs from clustered shafts in the walls; in the eastern half, on each side, are two tall windows of two lights, with most graceful tracery; at the east is a window of five lights, of equally beautiful tracery, filled with stained glass, of which the five lower figures are ancient and said to have been brought from Cologne. The west window has four lights. When Professor Willis was conducting some members of an architectural congress, in 1860,[77] over the monastic buildings, on arriving at this "beautiful little gem of architecture," in the course of his remarks "he pointed to the restorations that had taken place, and found that they were good ones, the actual mason's lines having been taken in some instances. In one or two cases where the work was destroyed the spaces had been filled up with plain block, purposely to show where the masonry had been knocked away." Some curious tiling is to be seen on the altar platform: there are figures of Adam and Eve and numerous unusual designs. On no account should this chapel be left unvisited.

ELY PORTA, THE GREAT GATE OF THE MONASTERY, 1817.

From Stevenson's Supplement to Bentham.

ELY PORTA

[77] At which the writer was present.

The great gateway of the abbey, **Ely Porta**, remains in a nearly perfect condition. It was the place where the manor courts were held, and was in course of erection when Prior Bucton died in 1397. From his successor, in whose time it seems to have been completed, it is sometimes called Walpole's gate. At one time a portion was devoted to the brewery, and here the audit ale was brewed till so recently as Dean Goodwin's time.[78] It is now used partly as a house for the porter and partly for the school. The new buildings of the school, just opposite, are on the site of an ancient hostelry called the Green Man, which was "possibly the descendant of some mediæval lodging-house to which pilgrims resorted."[79]

Between Ely Porta and the cathedral are to be seen many fragmentary remains of the old monastery, some of Norman date, now forming parts of houses. Over the road to the west of these buildings there used to be a covered passage, called "The Gallery"—a name still retained by the street itself—leading from the bishop's palace to the cathedral. Access to this from the cathedral was in the western transept. The writer has not been able to hear of any engraving or drawing of this.

The remains of the refectory and of the Norman kitchen are in the deanery grounds. The guest-house is wholly absorbed in the deanery. There is a picturesque entrance into the close, on the north side, from High Street. The buildings on each side of it and the room above (now the muniment room) are quite ecclesiastical, though modernised and in part new. The eastern portion occupies the site of the sextry.

---

[78] "Ely Gossip," p. 5.
[79] *Ib.*, p. 7.

DIMENSIONS OF ELY CATHEDRAL.

Length (interior)	517 feet.
Length of nave	230 feet.
Width of nave	78 feet.
Width of octagon	74 feet.
Height of vault	72 feet.
Height of western tower	215 feet.
Area	46,000 sq. feet.

1. S. Edmund's Chapel.
2. Bishop Alcock's Chapel.
3. Bishop West's Chapel.
4. Cardinal Luxemburg.
5. Bishop Allen.
6. Canon Mill.
7. Bishop Hothain.
8. Tiptoft, Earl of Worcester.
9. Bishop Barnet.
10. Bishop Louth.
11. Bishop Goodrich (brass).
12. Dean Tyndall (brass).
13. Bishop Heton.
14. Bishop Gunning.
15. Canon Selwyn.
16. Bishop Redman.
17. Bishop Kilkenny.
18. Shrine of S. Etheldreda.
19. Bishop Northwold.
20. Bishop Sparke.

NORMAN

EARLY ENGLISH

DECORATED

PERPENDICULAR

MODERN

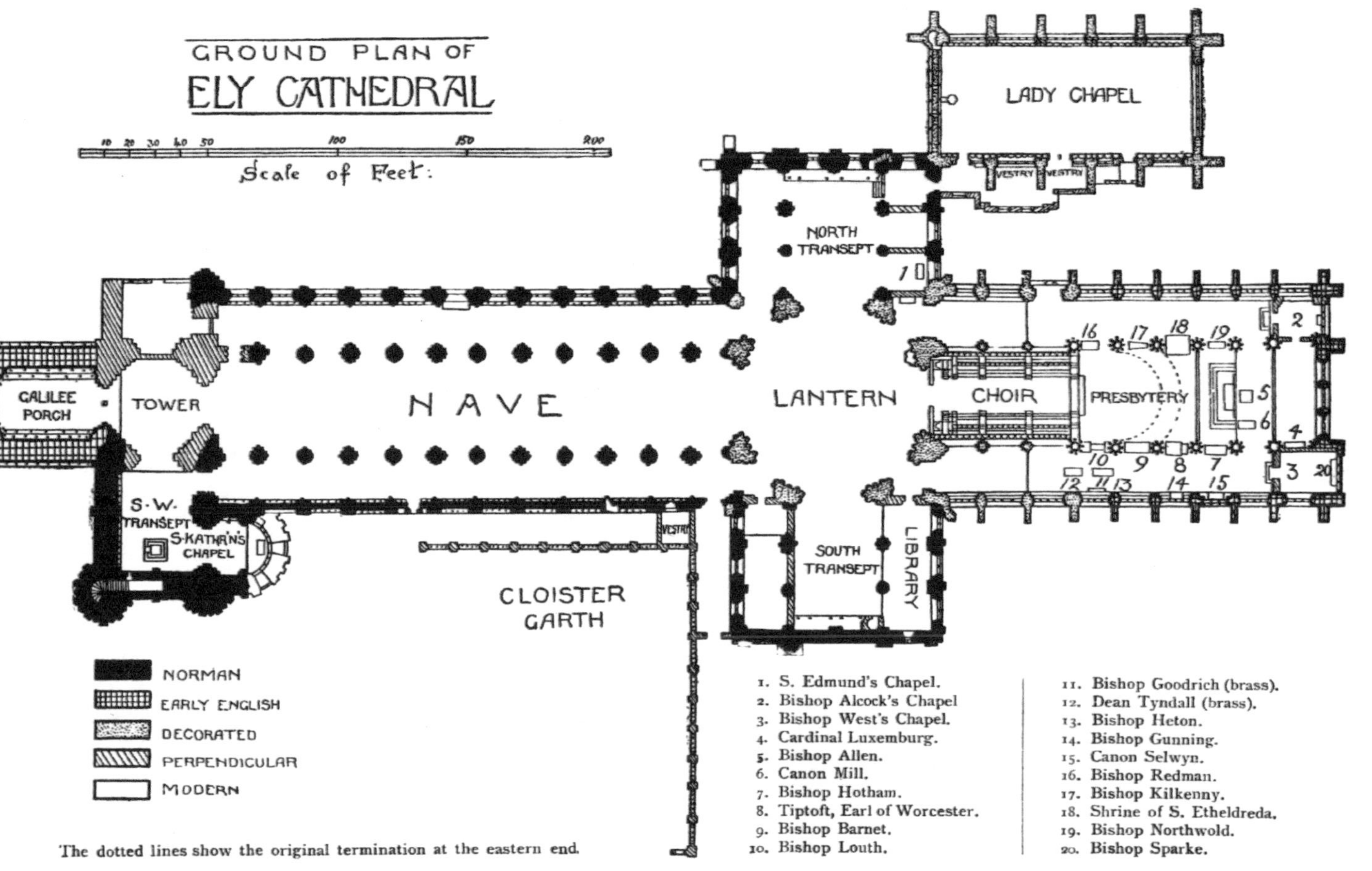

GROUND PLAN OF
ELY CATHEDRAL
Scale of Feet:
10 20 30 40 50 100 150 200
LADY CHAPEL
VESTRY VESTRY
NORTH TRANSEPT
NAVE
LANTERN
CHOIR
PRESBYTERY
GALILEE PORCH
TOWER
S.W. TRANSEPT
S. KATHN'S CHAPEL
CLOISTER GARTH
VESTRY
SOUTH TRANSEPT
LIBRARY
NORMAN
EARLY ENGLISH
DECORATED
PERPENDICULAR
MODERN
1. S. Edmund's Chapel.
2. Bishop Alcock's Chapel
3. Bishop West's Chapel.
4. Cardinal Luxemburg.
5. Bishop Allen.
6. Canon Mill.
7. Bishop Hotham.
8. Tiptoft, Earl of Worcester.
9. Bishop Barnet.
10. Bishop Louth.
11. Bishop Goodrich (brass).
12. Dean Tyndall (brass).
13. Bishop Heton.
14. Bishop Gunning.
15. Canon Selwyn.
16. Bishop Redman.
17. Bishop Kilkenny.
18. Shrine of S. Etheldreda.
19. Bishop Northwold.
20. Bishop Sparke.
The dotted lines show the original termination at the eastern end.

INDEX.

A

B

T

W

Lector House believes that a society develops through a two-fold approach of continuous learning and adaptation, which is derived from the study of classic literary works spread across the historic timeline of literature records. Therefore, we aim at reviving, repairing and redeveloping all those inaccessible or damaged but historically as well as culturally important literature across subjects so that the future generations may have an opportunity to study and learn from past works to embark upon a journey of creating a better future.

This book is a result of an effort made by Lector House towards making a contribution to the preservation and repair of original ancient works which might hold historical significance to the approach of continuous learning across subjects.

HAPPY READING & LEARNING!

LECTOR HOUSE LLP
E-MAIL: lectorpublishing@gmail.com